Better Homes and Gardens®

CHRISTMAS
❧ FROM THE HEART ❧

VOLUME 8

Better Homes and Gardens Crafts Collection™
Des Moines, Iowa

Better Homes and Gardens®

CHRISTMAS FROM THE HEART®
VOLUME NO. 8

EDITOR-IN-CHIEF Beverly Rivers

MANAGING EDITOR Matthew T. Jones   ART DIRECTOR Daniel Masini

EDITOR Heidi Palkovic

EDITORIAL COORDINATOR Carol Moorlach

ADMINISTRATIVE ASSISTANT Shari Smith

CONTRIBUTING GRAPHIC DESIGNER Kimberly Zarley

CONTRIBUTING ILLUSTRATORS
Glenda Aldrich, Barbara J. Gordon, Roxanne LeMoine
Chris Neubauer Graphics, Carson Ode, Carrie Topp

CONTRIBUTING PHOTO STYLIST Ann Blevins

PUBLISHER William R. Reed

MARKETING DIRECTOR Maureen Ruth

MARKETING MANAGER Andre Okolowitz

PROMOTION SUPERVISOR M. Max Wilker

BUSINESS MANAGER Cathy Bellis

PRODUCTION DIRECTOR Douglas M. Johnston

PRODUCTION MANAGER Pam Kvitne

ASSISTANT PREPRESS MANAGER Marjorie J. Schenkelberg

VICE PRESIDENT, PUBLISHING DIRECTOR Jerry Ward

CHAIRMAN AND CEO William T. Kerr

CHAIRMAN OF THE EXECUTIVE COMMITTEE E.T. Meredith III

MEREDITH PUBLISHING GROUP

PUBLISHING GROUP PRESIDENT Christopher M. Little

FOR BOOK EDITORIAL QUESTIONS, WRITE:
Better Homes and Gardens®, Christmas From the Heart®
1716 Locust St., Des Moines, IA 50309-3023

COVER PHOTOGRAPH: Marcia Cameron

ISSN: 1081-4698
ISBN: 0-696 20899-7

$\mathcal{W}$hen we make beautiful handcrafts for holiday gifts and celebrations, each loving stitch, brushstroke, and craft work says that ours is a CHRISTMAS FROM THE HEART.

Paint a quick and easy papier mâché gift box with a cheery holiday message. See the instructions on page 155.

CONTENTS

TOY EMPORIUM

194

MERRY CHRISTMAS

HOME
🌿 FOR THE HOLIDAYS 🌿

When your family gathers

to celebrate the season, share your crafts along

with the cheer. Traditional plaid motifs prevail

on ribbon-decked greenery and painted dinnerware,

and festive reds and greens grace painted floral

ornaments and a patchwork stocking. Creative table

favors, ribbon-wrapped packages, a nostalgic cross-

stitch picture and more will make your gathering

a tradition the family eagerly anticipates.

Instructions begin on page 22.

PLAID-RIBBONS DINNERWARE

In keeping with a red-plaid decorating theme, paint plaid holiday ribbons on glass plates, platters, goblets, and mugs. Vibrant Christmas colors and easy, repeated patterns make the dishes a beautiful addition to your holiday table. Instructions are on page 29.

LACY DOILY ORNAMENT

A paper-lace doily gets a whole new look as an elegant cornucopia ornament for your tree. Adorned with pretty ribbons and filled with wrapped candies, these lovely little ornaments are a welcome addition to your tree. Instructions are on page 35.

YULE LOG CRATE

While waiting for Santa to slide down your chimney, store your yule logs beside the hearth in this cheery painted crate. Bold, bright colors and wooden cutout shapes offer a delightful "Merry Christmas" to all—especially Santa. Instructions are on page 39.

WRAPPED-IN-RIBBONS PACKAGES

Give your gifts a personal flair by wrapping them in ribbons. An assortment of plaid and mesh ribbons combined with cordings makes your gift presentation unique. Instructions are on page 41.

$\mathcal{S}$HIMMERING SNOWFLAKE STOCKING

Achieve a "woven" fabric effect for this elegant stocking with squares of velveteen fabric. Cross-stitch a flurry of snowflakes on the cuff to complete the festive look. Instructions are on page 36.

FLYING ST. NICK

Set a side table with traditional holiday treats and a hand-painted folk art St. Nick. Our joyous "flying" figure sports a horn to herald the arrival of the season. Instructions are on page 23.

CORDING-COVERED ORNAMENTS

Turn a simple plastic-foam ball or cone into an elegant decoration for your tree. With just a few wraps of cording and a touch of gilded ornamental fruit, these creative cone and ball trims are quick-and-easy holiday crafts. Instructions are on page 25 and 33.

ELEGANT VELVET STOCKINGS

Craft heirloom stockings your family will cherish for many
holidays to come. The cuffs on our pair are banded with
luxurious trims and decorative buttons.
Instructions are on page 33.

SNAPPER CRACKER FAVORS

Delight your party guests with these
holiday favorites influenced by British tradition. Our
handmade snapper cracker favors suit country, Victorian,
and contemporary tastes. Simply accent with raffia and
holly berries, pearls and lace, or gold-ribbon ties. Or make
some snapper cracker favors just for kids, including a set of
Jacks game pieces. Instructions are on page 40.

GILDED-PEAR LAMPSHADE AND PLACE CARDS

Grace a mantel with a stylish lampshade and top your table with simple place cards depicting our stamped gilded-pear motif. Instructions are on page 32.

MESH-RIBBON ORNAMENT

Lacy-looking mesh ribbon turns a plain-glass or plastic-ball ornament into a quick-to-make tree decoration. Instructions are on page 36.

CHRISTMAS WISHES CROSS-STITCH PICTURE

Recall the joys of wishing for holiday toys while cross-stitching our heartwarming "Toy Emporium" picture. Give it as a gift to make someone's holiday wish come true! Instructions are on page 25.

TRADITIONAL PLAID WREATH AND GARLAND

Spruce up your home this holiday using greenery dressed with twists
of red-plaid fabrics. Wreath and garland projects assemble quickly,
coordinate wonderfully, and display traditional beauty.
Instructions are on page 40.

RIBBON-DECKED CANDY PLATE

Apply woven ribbons to the bottom of a
glass plate for an attractive Christmas candy
dish. Instructions are on page 30.

SILK LEAVES ORNAMENT

Fashion this fabulous ornament fast—just glue festive silk leaves onto a plastic-foam ball and add a gold-ribbon accent for a hanger. Instructions are on page 39.

FESTIVE FLORAL ORNAMENTS

Trim your tree with a "garden" of fabulous painted floral ornaments. With a few simple freehand strokes, these glass-ball decorations are quick to make so you can use them as gifts or to deck your own tree. Instructions are on page 34.

GLISTENING CROSS-STITCH ORNAMENTS

Using metallic ribbons and sparkling crystals, these traditional red-and-green geometric cross-stitch creations will look dazzling on your tree. You'll cherish these ornaments, which are finished onto a square backing and adorned with a cording trim and a hanger. Instructions are on page 30.

FLYING ST. NICK PATTERNS

¼" hole
¼" deep

Belt placement

Make two

FLYING ST. NICK
Shown on page 13 *and* below.

YOU WILL NEED:

Patterns on pages 22 *and* 24

Tracing paper

¾×5×9" pine

½×4×7" pine

¼×1×3" Baltic birch plywood

⅛×1×2" Baltic birch plywood

Scrollsaw and #5 blade

Drill and ¼" drill bit

100- and 150-grit sandpaper and tack cloth

Wood sealer

Loew-Cornell brushes: #10 synthetic flat, #6 synthetic flat, #2 synthetic flat, #1 synthetic liner, ⅜" synthetic angular shader, ¼" flat stippling brush

DecoArt Americana Colors Acrylic paint: Antique Rose DA156 (AR), Buttermilk DA3 (BK), Deep Burgundy DA128 (DB), Deep Midnight Blue DA166 (DM), Driftwood DA171 (DW), French Gray Blue DA98 (FB), Flesh Tone DA78 (FT), Hauser Dark Green DA133 (HD), Black Plum DA172 (KP), Lamp Black DA67 (LB), Mississippi Mud DA94 (MM), Moon Yellow DA7 (MY), Shading Flesh DA137 (SF), Raw Umber DA130 (RW), and True Ochre DA143 (TR)

4½" length of ¼"-diameter dowel

2¾" wood cube

¾" wood bead with ¼"-diameter hole

2" wood wheel with ¼"-diameter hole

DecoArt Dazzling Metallics paint: Glorious Gold DA71 (GG)

Matte finish spray and 5-minute epoxy

4½" of bead-twist gold cord

INSTRUCTIONS

Trace the patterns. Copy the outlines of the Santa head, body, and feet onto ¾" pine, the two arms and the star onto ½" pine, the horn onto ¼" Baltic birch plywood, and the mustache onto ⅛" plywood.

Cut out the shapes with a scrollsaw, using a #5 blade. Drill the two ¼" holes as shown on the pattern. Sand all surfaces with 100- and then 150-grit sandpaper. Remove the sanding dust with a tack cloth.

Apply wood sealer to all surfaces, and let the sealer dry. Sand again with 150-grit sandpaper, and wipe clean with a tack cloth. Copy the main pattern lines onto the Santa and cube.

Base-coat with the #10, #6, and #2 flat brushes, choosing the size that best fits the area. The #2 flat brush is also used for tapping in the evergreens. Use the #1 liner for details, and the ⅜" angular shader for float-shading. Use the stippling brush to apply the fur.

Base-coat the face FT; the mouth AR; the horn and the top and bottom surfaces of the star TR; the beard, mustache piece, the dowel, the snowy ground area on the cube, and the snowmen BK; the eyebrows and fur on the Santa robe and the house (excluding the roof) on the cube DW. Mix FB and BK 1:2, and base-coat the pond, then mix DW and BK 1:1 and base-coat the path. Base-coat the mittens and the top of the cube and sky area FB; and the boots, house windows, and the ¾" bead DM. Base-coat the 2" wheel, the door and chimneys on the house, the tiny birds on the cube, and Santa's robe and sleeves DB; and the edges of the star MY. Base-coat the house roof and the birdhouse MM, using RW and LB mixed 2:1 to line the trees and the post, roof, and base of the birdhouse. Tap in the evergreens with the #2 flat brush, using HD. Pick up a bit of LB with the HD occasionally to shade, and a bit of TR to highlight. Repeat the house and birdhouse scenes on the remaining two cube sides.

Line the nose and shade the face SF. Float the cheeks with AR, and deepen slightly with an additional float of DB. Base-coat the eyes BK, add a DM iris, and highlight the iris at the lower part with a floated half-circle of FB. Use LB to line the top of the eye and paint the eyelashes. Paint BK shine marks on the eyes, tip of the nose, the mouth, and the cheeks as shown on the pattern.

FLYING ST. NICK PATTERNS

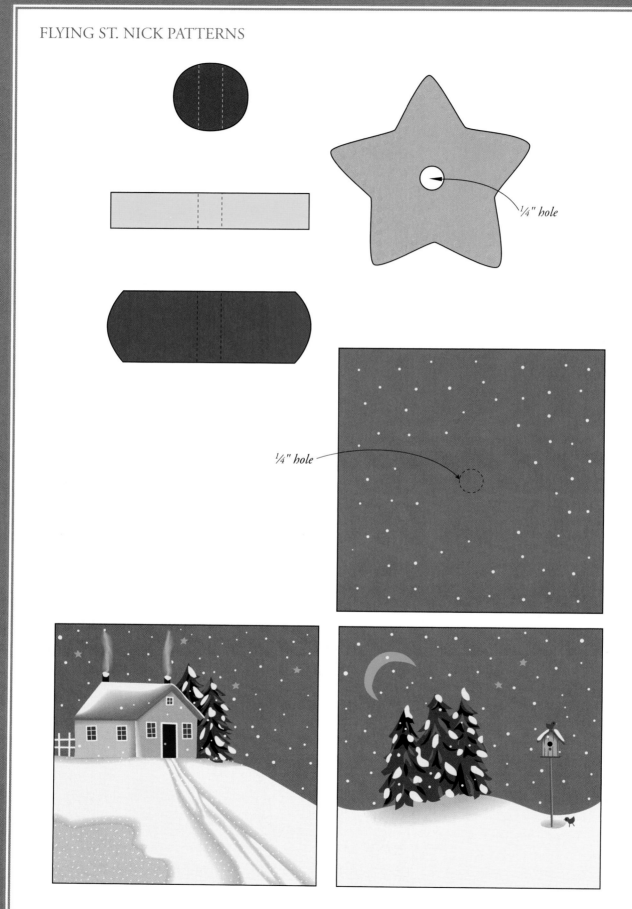

¼" hole

¼" hole

Shade the horn with RW, then highlight the bell of the horn with MY and paint shine marks with BK. Float a shade on the mittens with DM, and highlight the boots with floated FB. Mix DM and LB 2:1, and shade the boots. Float the shading on the robe with KP, and highlight with AR. Paint pulled-out dot stars on the robe with thinned-to-ink consistency TR, and add the BK dots. Dot the buttons on the robe, the shoe buttons on the boots, and the dots on the star top side with GG; when the robe and boot dots are dry, repeat so they are slightly raised. Stipple BK on the fur and eyebrows. Use DW to shade and line the beard and mustache and to stipple the shading on the fur.

Shade the snow with the FB and BK 1:2 mix, and dot the birdhouse openings with LB. With BK, line the fence, windows, and doors, dot the snow in the sky, streak the icy pond, and paint the clumps of snow on all the objects as shown. Dry-brush a dusting of snow on the roof of the house with BK. Float shading on the house with MM and a highlight with DW and BK mixed 1:1. The chimney smoke is painted with thinned BK. Paint the moon and stars and the birds' bills with TR.

Apply one or more coats of matte finish spray to all surfaces, allowing ample drying time between coats.

Sand off the paint where the pieces will join, and attach the arms (attach one arm to the back side of the figure) and the horn with 5-minute epoxy. Push the dowel into the cube, then first slide the wheel, then the star, and then the bead on the dowel down to the cube. Glue the Santa on top of the dowel and the cord around his waist for a belt.

—Designed by Nelda Rice

CHRISTMAS WISHES CROSS-STITCH PICTURE

Shown on page 17 *and* below.
The design size is 11½×8¼".

YOU WILL NEED:

Chart on page 26
19×16" piece of 28-count Black Monaco fabric
Size 24 tapestry needle
Cotton embroidery floss in the colors listed in the key on *page 27*

INSTRUCTIONS

Zigzag-stitch or overcast the edges of the fabric to prevent fraying. Find the center of the chart and the center of the fabric; begin stitching there.

Use three plies of floss to work the cross-stitches and three-quarter cross-stitches over two threads of the fabric. Work backstitches using the number of plies of floss as indicated in the color key on *page 27*. Work the blended-needle stitches as specified in the key. Work the French knots using one ply of floss wrapped twice around the embroidery needle.

Press the finished stitchery from the back. Frame the piece as desired.

—Designed by Barbara Core

CORDING-COVERED BALL ORNAMENT

Shown on page 13.
The ornament is 3½" in diameter.

YOU WILL NEED:

Offray Ribbon cords and trims: 3½ yards of 5⁄16"-diameter beaded Red/Green Cord, 30" of 3⁄16"-diameter Gold Morocco Cord, and 3—1¼"-diameter Gold Small Blooming Roses
Glue gun
Hotmelt adhesive
3"-diameter plastic-foam ball

INSTRUCTIONS

Adhere one end of the Beaded Red/Green Cord to the bottom of the plastic-foam ball. Coil, wrap, and glue the cord around the ball.

Glue one end of the Gold Morocco Cord to the top of the ball. Referring to the photograph on *page 13,* bend the cord into five continuous 2"-long leaves. Pin the tips of the leaves to the sides and the opposite ends of the leaves to the top of the ball.

Form a loop with the excess cord, gluing the end to the top of the ball. Pin roses to the top of the ball.

—Designed by Ellie Joos

"CHRISTMAS WISHES" CROSS-STITCH PICTURE CHART

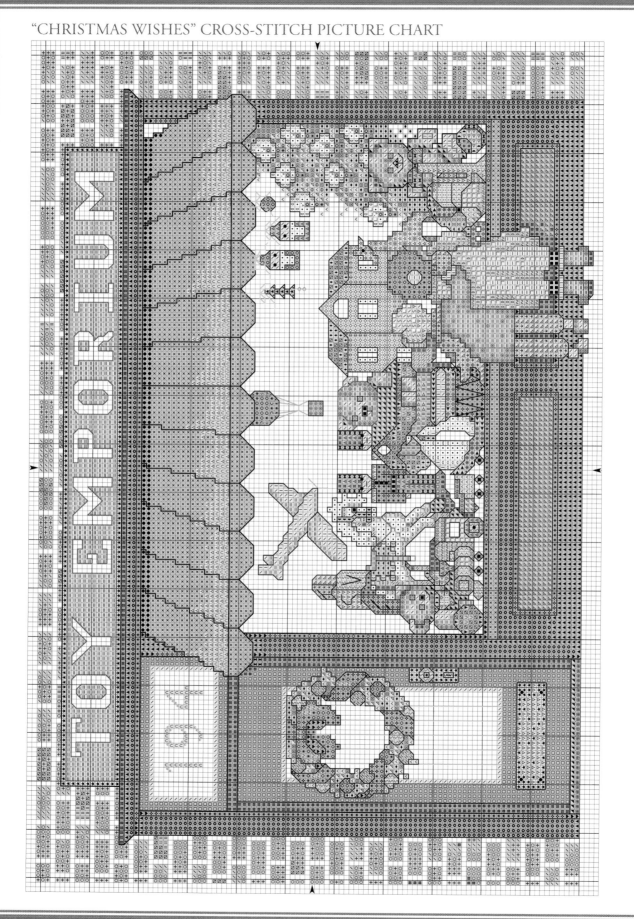

TOY EMPORIUM

Anchor		DMC	
002	●	000	White
110	◖	208	Dark lavender
109	✹	209	Medium lavender
108	⊠	210	Light lavender
403	■	310	Black
979	◀	312	Light navy
399	◳	318	Light steel
9046	✳	321	True Christmas red
978	⊕	322	Pale navy
977	★	334	Dark baby blue
013	◍	349	Dark coral
011	◈	350	Medium coral
010	◠	351	Light coral
009	◰	352	Pale coral
008	−	353	Peach
1014	⊞	355	Dark terra-cotta
5975	⊘	356	Medium terra-cotta
401	◢	413	Pewter
235	⊞	414	Dark steel
398	♡	415	Light pearl gray
358	⌗	433	Dark chestnut
310	☐	434	Medium chestnut
1046	◤	435	Light chestnut
1045	◉	436	Dark tan
362	⊟	437	Medium tan
1005	✤	498	Dark Christmas red
212	☒	561	Dark seafoam
210	∩	562	Medium seafoam
926	⌒	712	Cream
361	◺	738	Light tan
885	❘	739	Pale tan
314	▽	741	Medium tangerine
302	◁	743	True yellow
300	⌐	745	Light yellow
158	◇	747	Light sky blue
234	⌣	762	Pale pearl gray
133	⋈	796	Medium royal blue
132	⌗	797	Light royal blue
131	△	798	Dark Delft blue
136	◿	799	Medium Delft blue
359	✕	801	Medium coffee brown
043	♥	815	Garnet
1044	◆	895	Dark hunter green
360	◉	898	Dark coffee brown
1014	◆	919	Red-copper
340	◲	920	Medium copper
338	‖	921	True copper
1003	▷	922	Light copper
381	▲	938	Deep coffee brown
187	⋈	958	True aqua
186	▷	959	Medium aqua
076	◗	961	Dark rose-pink
075	◁	962	Medium rose-pink
073	⁞	963	Pale rose-pink
246	▼	986	Dark forest green
244	⊘	987	Medium forest green
243	⋃	988	Light forest green
410	▶	995	Dark electric blue
433	⊛	996	Medium electric blue
268	⊡	3345	Medium hunter green
267	⊖	3346	Light hunter green
266	◰	3347	Medium yellow-green
264	∧	3348	Light yellow-green
025	♡	3716	Light rose-pink
140	◺	3755	Medium baby blue
928	◫	3761	Medium sky blue
306	★	3820	Dark straw
305	▽	3821	True straw
874	⑤	3822	Light straw
5975	◎	3830	True terra-cotta

BLENDED NEEDLE

010	Ⓓ	351	Light coral (2X) and
009		352	Pale coral (1X)
358	◩	433	Dark chestnut (2X) and
310		434	Medium chestnut (1X)
212	△	561	Dark seafoam (2X) and
210		562	Medium seafoam (1X)
212	●	561	Dark seafoam (2X) and
403		310	Black (1X)
302	☆	743	True yellow (2X) and
303		742	Light tangerine (1X)

BACKSTITCH

110	╱	208	Dark lavender – reins on horse (2X)
9046	╱	321	True Christmas red – "Toy Emporium" and inner border of the sign (2X)
362	╱	437	Medium tan – saddle stirrup (2X)
361	╱	738	Light tan – bars in door, airplane propeller (2X); balloon with basket (1X)
043	╱	815	Garnet – girl's coat, candles in tree (1X)
382	╱	3371	Black-brown – teddy bear under tree, and bear in corner (1X)
306	╱	3820	Dark straw – strings on hanging ornaments (1X)
403	╱	310	Black – outer edge of Toy Emporium sign, awning, top of building and fluted edge, outer edge of door, window edge (2X); all remaining stitches (1X)

FRENCH KNOT

403	●	310	Black – bolts on door plate, train wheels, soldier's uniform buttons, hanging ornaments' eyes, giraffe's eye, soldier's eyes
885	◦	739	Pale tan – bears' eyes
306	◦	3820	Dark straw – bell ringers

Stitch count: *113 high x 172 wide*

Finished design sizes:
28-count fabric – 8 x 12⅛ inches
32-count fabric – 7 x 10¾ inches
36-count fabric – 6⅛ x 9½ inches

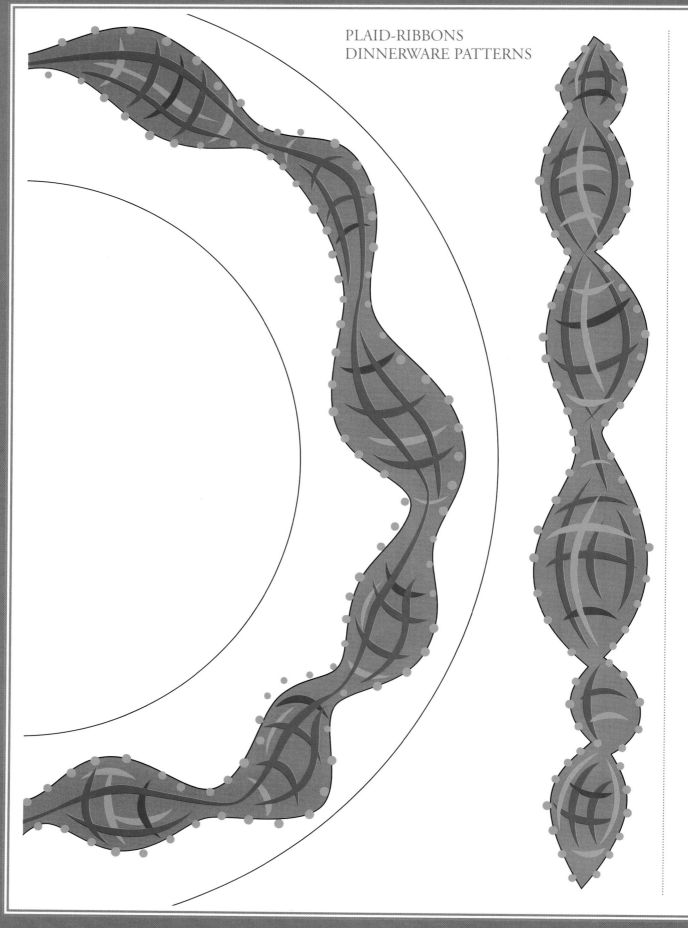

PLAID-RIBBONS
DINNERWARE PATTERNS

PLAID-RIBBONS DINNERWARE PATTERN

PLAID-RIBBONS DINNERWARE

Shown on pages 8, 9, *and* 14.

YOU WILL NEED:

Patterns opposite *and* above

Glass plates, pedestal mugs, bowl, goblets,
  and platters
Tracing paper
Pencil, scissors, and stylus
Repositionable stencil adhesive
Loew-Cornell Series 7000 brushes: #5 round
  and #1 liner
Liquitex Glossies paint: Blue 013, Gold 051,
  Green 011, and Red 017
Palette or disposable plastic plate
Water container

INSTRUCTIONS

Note: *When working with glass, make
sure your hands are clean and free of
hand lotion and oil.*

Wash the glassware with warm
soapy water or a mixture of water and
vinegar to remove dirt and oils.
Towel the glassware dry.

Trace the patterns onto tracing
paper, and cut them to fit the

Base-coat ribbon trim with Red.

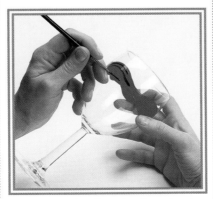

Apply plaid details with a liner brush.

surfaces. Spray the patterns with
stencil adhesive and smooth them
onto the top of the plate and platter

rims and the inner surface of the
bowl, pedestal mugs, and goblets.

To paint platters, bowls, and
stemware in different sizes, cut
additional patterns, and then position
and adhere them to the surfaces in a
pleasing arrangement.

For bowls, mugs, and goblets, paint
the ribbon area with Red using a
round brush. Make sure there is very
little water in your brush. The paint
covers the glass much better when it's
applied full-strength. Use an ample
amount of paint on your brush, and
don't overstroke wet areas too much
or you may wipe off or smear the
paint you've applied. One coat of
paint is adequate.

Paint the plaid details with the
remaining colors using the liner
brush. Refer to the photographs on
pages 8, 9, and *14* for placement.

For descending "dip dots," dip the
end of a stylus into the gold paint,
and set it down on the widest area of
the ribbon. Continue applying dots
until you reach a narrow area. Then
dip the stylus into paint again and
continue applying the dots, beginning
where the ribbon is widest.

To paint the plates and platters,
apply the plaid details and the dots
first. Let the paint dry. Then paint
the ribbon with red.

Remove the patterns and clean the
adhesive residue carefully with soap
and water.

Place the glassware in a cold oven.
Heat the oven to 325° and bake for
30 to 45 minutes.

Turn the oven off, but don't remove
the glassware until the oven and
glassware are cool.

Although the glassware should be
dishwasher safe, we recommend
washing it by hand.

—*Designed by Ann Blevins*

RIBBON-DECKED CANDY PLATE

Shown on page 18.
The plate measures 8" in diameter.

YOU WILL NEED:

2 yards each of 1"-wide red sheer (RS) and
  green sheer (GS) ribbon
3 yards of 5/8"-wide plaid (P) ribbon
6 yards of 3/16"-wide gold-edged red (R) ribbon
14" (or larger) square of foam-core board
Clear plastic wrap
T-pins
Masking tape
8"-diameter clear glass plate with gold rim
Glass cleaner
Mod Podge
Disposable foam brush

INSTRUCTIONS

Cut all of the ribbons into 12" lengths. Wrap the foam-core board with the clear plastic wrap. Arrange the ribbons lengthwise on the wrapped board, using T-pins to hold them in place. Position the ribbons from left to right as follows: RS, R, P, R, RS, R, P, R, GS, R, P, R, RS, R, P, R, GS. Pin the ribbons so they touch one another.

Starting 1" from the top edge, begin weaving the crosswise ribbons as follows: RS, R, P, R, GS, R, P, R, RS, R, P, R, GS, R, P, R, RS. Adhere the woven-ribbon square to the plastic wrap with masking tape.

Clean the plate with the glass cleaner, and allow it to dry. With the plate face down on a flat work surface, apply Mod Podge to the wrong side of the plate with the foam brush. Apply Mod Podge to the woven-ribbon square. Remove the T-pins, and place the woven-ribbon square with the Mod Podge side facing up to the wrong side of the plate. Remove the tape and the plastic wrap. Adjust the woven ribbons along the curves of the plate, smoothing out all bubbles. Add more Mod Podge as necessary so the ribbons are entirely covered. Allow to dry. If a thicker decoupage covering is desired, brush on another coat of Mod Podge and allow it to dry.

Carefully cut away any extra ribbon around the edge of the plate.

—Designed by Margaret Sindelar

GLISTENING CROSS-STITCH ORNAMENTS

Shown on page 21 *and* above.
Each ornament is 4" square.

YOU WILL NEED:

Charts opposite

For each ornament:
5¼"-square of 26-count Silver Lurex
  Jobelan fabric
Cotton embroidery floss, Metallic ribbon, and
  Mill Hill seed beads as listed in the key
  opposite
Mill Hill Silver Star Glass Treasure 12061
Kreinik 001 Silver #4 very fine braid
Embroidery hoop
Size 24 tapestry needle
Beading needle
Tacky glue
Scissors
2—4"-squares of cardboard
2—4"-squares of fleece
Cotton embroidery floss in red and green

INSTRUCTIONS

Zigzag-stitch or overcast the edges of the fabric to prevent fraying. Find the center of the chart *opposite* and the center of the fabric; begin stitching there. Use three plies of floss to work the cross-stitches over two threads of the fabric. Use one ply of each color of floss for blended-needle stitches.

To make the straight stitches using the metallic ribbon, bring the ribbon up through the fabric at one corner as indicated on the chart. Bring it down through the fabric at the next corner, keeping the ribbon from twisting with the opposite hand and adjusting tension. Make another straight stitch to the next corner and continue around all four sides. To hold the ribbon in place, tack it down with silver braid using small running stitches through both ribbon and fabric all the way around the ornament. Secure the ends. Attach the beads with a half cross-stitch using two strands of matching floss.

Make Ornament #1 (the herringbone pattern) as follows. Using the emerald metallic ribbon, make large cross-stitches around the inner diamond shape. See the top chart *opposite* for details. Use the index finger of your other hand to keep ribbon from twisting when making the stitches. Beginning in the upper left-hand corner of the design, work the outer border in herringbone stitch using one ply of shaded thread. Sew a glass star in the center.

Make Ornament #2 (the Smyrna cross-stitch border) as follows. Using the green metallic ribbon, work straight stitches around the inner green diamond border. Use the index finger of your opposite hand to keep ribbon from twisting while stitching. See bottom chart *opposite* for details.

GLISTENING CROSS-STITCH
ORNAMENTS CHARTS

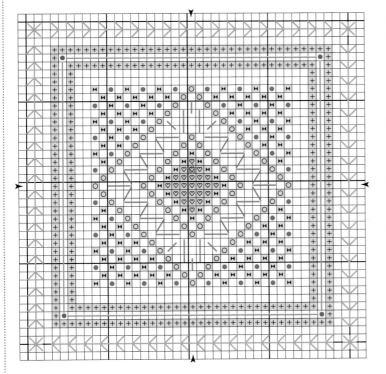

SQUARE ORNAMENT # 1

Anchor		DMC	
	⋈	321	Christmas red
	♡	550	Violet
	◎	3818	Emerald green
	+	Caron Collection floss 032	Passion Wildflowers

STRAIGHT STITCH

	—	001HL	Silver metallic ⅟₁₆" ribbon
	—	009HL	Emerald metallic ⅟₁₆" ribbon

HERRINGBONE STITCH

	✕	Caron Collection Floss 032	Passion Wildflowers

ATTACHMENTS

	●	02010	Ice seed bead
	●	03043	Oriental red seed bead
	☆	12061	Crystal five-pointed star Glass Treasures

Stitch count: *41 high x 41 wide*

Finished design sizes:
26-count fabric – 1⁹⁄₁₆ x 1⁹⁄₁₆ inches
28-count fabric – 1⁷⁄₁₆ x 1⁷⁄₁₆ inches
32-count fabric – 1¼ x 1¼ inches

SQUARE ORNAMENT #2

Anchor		DMC	
9046	⋈	321	Christmas red
102	♡	550	Violet
923	◎	3818	Emerald green
	+	Caron Collection floss 032	Passion Wildflowers

STRAIGHT STITCH

923	—	3818	Emerald green
	—	001HL	Silver ⅟₁₆" ribbon
	—	009HL	Emerald ⅟₁₆" ribbon

BACKSTITCH

	/	Caron Collection floss 032	Passion Wildflowers

SMYRNA CROSS-STITCH

	✳	Caron Collection floss 032	Passion Wildflowers

ATTACHMENTS

	●	02010	Ice seed bead
	●	03043	Oriental red seed bead
	☆	12061	Crystal five-pointed star Glass Treasures

Stitch count: *41 high x 41 wide*

Finished design sizes:
26-count fabric – 1⁹⁄₁₆ x 1⁹⁄₁₆ inches
28-count fabric – 1⁷⁄₁₆ x 1⁷⁄₁₆ inches
32-count fabric – 1¼ x 1¼ inches

Use two strands of emerald green floss to make the straight stitches between the green metallic stitches. For the outer border, start in the upper left-hand corner by making a Smyrna cross-stitch with one ply of the shaded thread. Continue to the right, working the backstitch border to the right-hand corner. Make the next Smyrna cross; continue around the border. Sew a glass star in the center.

Glue one square piece of fleece to one side of a cardboard square. Put the finished design right side up on top of the fleece. Center the design and pull the edges of fabric to the back of the cardboard. Glue fabric edges to the cardboard all around, trimming any excess fabric at corners. Repeat these directions for the back of the ornament using a plain fabric square, wrapped and glued over a second piece of fleece and cardboard.

Glue wrong sides of the front and back of the ornament together, leaving the top edge unglued.

Make cording as follows. Unfold one skein of red floss. Fold the entire length in half; cut. Put one half aside for the second ornament. Take the remaining floss and fold it in half, and then into quarters. Repeat these instructions with a skein of green floss. Place the folded green and red floss together. Put glue at one end of the floss, and insert this end into the top center of the ornament. Let dry.

Gently begin to twist the red and green floss together. Place a line of glue along the ornament edge, and glue the twisted cording along the edge. Continue to twist and glue the cording along the entire edge.

At the top of the ornament, make a loop of the twisted cording. Tie an overhand knot. Trim excess cording to 1" below the knot. Put glue on these ends, and tuck them into the top opening of the ornament.

—Designed by Louise Young

GILDED-PEAR LAMPSHADE AND PLACE CARDS

Shown on pages 16, 17, and left. The folded place cards are each 3×5".

YOU WILL NEED:

Pattern below

For both projects:
Rubber Stampede Pear stamp A253F
Clear embossing ink pad
Gold embossing powder
Embossing heat tool
For the place cards:
Cream-colored card stock
Embossing marking pen
Tracing paper
For the lampshade:
12"-wide hexagonal lampshade
Leather punching tool
2⅓ yards of ⅜"-wide red velvet ribbon
Glue

GILDED-PEAR PLACE CARD PATTERN

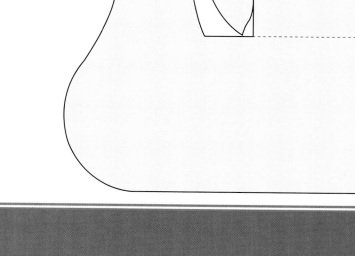

INSTRUCTIONS

For each place card, draw a 5×7" rectangle on the card stock. Don't cut out. Stamp the pear stamp to the lower left side of the card stock rectangles, using the embossing ink pad. Personalize the place cards with the embossing marking pen. Sprinkle the gold embossing powder over the stamped and written images. Shake the excess powder back into the jar.

Apply heat to the powder with an embossing heat tool to activate the powder. The stamped images will turn shiny gold and puff up a bit.

Trace the pattern onto tracing paper and cut it out. Align the traced and stamped pears, and pencil the pattern outline onto the stamped card stock. Cut and fold the place cards.

For ease in stamping the pear design on the lampshade, hold a sturdy support, such as a small book, inside each panel. Emboss the design in the center of each panel, following the directions for the place cards, above.

For the decorative lacing, lightly pencil a row of dots, evenly spaced, around the bottom of the lampshade. The dots on the lampshade are spaced at ½" intervals, ½" from the bottom edge. Using the leather punching tool, punch holes at each dot.

Trim the end of the ribbon on the diagonal, and thread the ribbon through the holes, overcasting the bottom edge of the lampshade. When the stitching is complete, glue the ribbon ends neatly to the interior of the lampshade.

—Designed by Ann Blevins

CORDING-COVERED CONE ORNAMENT

Shown on page 13 *and below left. The ornament, including the hanger, is 9" tall.*

YOU WILL NEED:

Plastic-foam cone
Sharp knife
Offray Cord and Ribbon: 4¼ yards of ⅛"-wide Wired Jazz Cord and ⅔ yard of 1½"-wide Gold Firefly/Magic Wand Ribbon
Glue gun and hotmelt adhesive
Spagum moss
Small artificial fruits, flowers, and silk leaves
Gold spray paint
Florist's wire and pick

INSTRUCTIONS

Trim the point from the plastic-foam cone, if necessary, so it measures about ¾" in diameter. Cut away the opposite end so the trimmed cone measures 4¼" tall.

Knot each end of the cord to keep it from unraveling. Glue one end of the cord to the center of the narrow end of the cone. Coil and glue the cord until the end is covered, then wrap and glue the cord around the cone all the way to the top. Glue a bit of moss to cover the top of the cone.

Spray gold paint on the fruits, flowers, and silk leaves. Let dry. Create a bow with 7" tails from the ribbon. Secure with florist's wire and a florist's pick. Set aside.

Referring to the photograph at *left,* glue the fruits, flowers, and leaves to the top of the cone. Add the ribbon bow. Drape one of the ribbon tails to the bottom front of the cone, and glue it in place.

Cut a 10"-length of the braid. Tie the braid into a bow and knot the ends. Glue to the bottom of the cone over the ribbon. Trim the other ribbon tail short, if desired.

Cut a 12" length of the cord and knot the ends. Glue the knots to each side of the cone for the hanger.

—Designed by Ellie Joos

ELEGANT VELVET STOCKINGS

Shown on page 15 *and below. Each stocking is 18" long.*

YOU WILL NEED:

Pattern on page 38

For each stocking:
Tracing paper
⅔ yard of red or green velvet
⅔ yard of thin fleece
⅔ yard of lining fabric
Matching sewing threads
1⅓ yards of ¼"-diameter coordinated cording
¼ yard of red or green velvet
½ yard each of 6 to 8 assorted trims
56 assorted decorative buttons
Large coordinated tassel

INSTRUCTIONS

Make the body of the stocking as follows. Trace the stocking pattern onto tracing paper. Add a ½" seam allowance all around the stocking. Cut out the completed pattern piece.

Cut a matching stocking front and back from the ⅔ yard of velvet, another set from the fleece, and a third set from the lining fabric.

Baste the fleece shapes to the wrong side of the velvet stocking front and back. With the right sides facing and using a ½" seam allowance, sew the stocking front to the back, leaving the top edge open. Clip the curves and turn the stocking right side out. Finger-press the seam.

Hand-sew the cording around the outside edge of the stocking.

Make the cuff as follows. Draw a 5×16" rectangle onto tracing paper for the cuff pattern. Add a ½" seam allowance all around the pattern. Cut out the completed pattern piece.

Cut out the cuff from the ¼ yard of velvet and a matching back from the lining fabric.

With the velvet cuff piece facing up, lay the trims across it in a pleasing arrangement. **Note:** *To make a wide band of trim, our designer sewed two trims close together, and covered the center seam with a narrow trim.* Hand-stitch the trims and buttons in place.

Fold the cuff in half crosswise with the right sides facing. Sew the short sides together. Finger-press the seam allowance open, and turn the cuff right side out.

Sew the lining piece in the same manner as directed for the velvet cuff, and finger-press the seam open. Slip the lining over the cuff

so the right sides are facing. Sew the pieces together around the bottom edge. Trim the seam allowance; turn the cuff right side out.

Finish the stocking as follows. Slip the lined cuff over the top of the stocking (with the cuff lining facing the right side of the stocking), matching the raw edges. Stitch the cuff to the stocking.

With the right sides facing, stitch the stocking lining pieces together, leaving the top edge open and leaving an opening along one side for turning. Don't turn right side out.

Slip the stocking into the lining with the right sides facing, and sew completely around the opening. Turn the stocking right side out through the opening in the lining.

Slip-stitch the opening closed, then tuck the lining inside the stocking.

Open out the cuff. Keeping the cuff free, topstitch through the stocking and the lining ¼" from the seam line around the top edge.

Turn down the cuff. Hand-stitch the tassel to the top inside right edge of the stocking cuff, stitching it close to the top of the tassel, and leaving the loop free so that it can be used as a hanging loop.

—Designed by Ann Blevins

FESTIVE FLORAL ORNAMENTS

Shown on page 20 *and below. Each ornament is 3" in diameter.*

YOU WILL NEED:

Delta Satin Finish PermEnamel paint: Ivory (IV), Maize (MZ), Chocolate (DC), Black, and 14K Gold (GO)
DecoArt Ultra Gloss Acrylic Enamel paint: Avocado (AV)
White plastic-foam plate
Delta PermEnamel Retarder
3"-diameter red or green frosted-glass ornaments
Paintbrushes: #4 liner and #8 filbert

INSTRUCTIONS

Place a dimesize puddle of each paint color on a white plastic-foam plate along with the retarder. **Note:** *Don't thin the paint with water.*

Refer to the photographs *opposite* to paint the flower blossom on the ornament. Dip the filbert brush into IV, and use two brush strokes to paint each petal, pulling both strokes toward the center of the flower. Let dry briefly.

Without washing the brush, dip it into MZ and DC. Tap the tip of the brush into the center of the flower, twisting to mix the colors. Dip the liner brush into DC and Black. Tap DC/Black dots into the center of the flower, and pull out tiny irregular lines. Make Black dots around the flower center. If desired, add a thin layer of IV to lighten the flower edges and tips. Use a thin wash of GO to highlight the flower.

Dip the filbert brush into equal parts of MZ and AV.

Mix the two colors together, using the tip of the brush. Press the paint-filled brush to the outside edge of a flower petal. Lift the brush,

Pull two brushstrokes per petal toward the center of the flower.

Tap Chocolate and Black dots into the flower center.

Spatter the painted piece with Ivory.

twisting it slightly, to form half a leaf. Do this twice to make a complete leaf. Rinse and dry the brush well.

Dip the brush into AV, MZ, and IV. Mix the colors together with the tip of the brush, then highlight the top half of the leaf. Paint two or three leaves for each flower.

Using the tip of the liner brush, mix AV, MZ, and IV. Twist and pull the paint slightly on the palette to make a good point on the brush. Loosely holding the brush, paint a curlicue and a stem. Use the brush to mix AV, MZ, and IV. Press, lift, and twist the brush to make three to five small leaves along the stem.

Dip the toothbrush into IV. Remove excess paint by pressing the toothbrush gently on a clean plastic-foam plate. Hold the toothbrush with the bristles up. Pull the bristles backward with your thumb, causing the paint to spatter away from you and onto the ornament.

—Designed by Rebecca Schlueter

LACY DOILY ORNAMENT
Shown on page 8 and below.
The finished ornament is 7½" tall.

YOU WILL NEED:

Offray Ribbons: 20" length of 4"-wide Red Sea Maid Ribbon, ¾ yard of ⅛"-wide Red Rose Garland (with 14 roses), 1⅓ yards of ⅛"-wide Red Dainty Double-face Satin Ribbon, and 8" of ¼"-wide Red Double-face Satin Ribbon
Glue gun and hotmelt adhesive
Spray adhesive
2—6"-diameter gold paper doilies
Compass and pinking shears
10" of gold bead trim
Florist's wire and plastic foam
Wrapped candies

INSTRUCTIONS

Piece the 4"-wide ribbon together with hotmelt adhesive to make a 7" square. Spray adhesive onto the back of one gold doily. Center and press it onto the red-ribbon square. Spray and press the other doily to the other side of the red-ribbon square. Using a compass, draw a 6"-diameter circle on the doily. Cut out the circle with the pinking shears.

Wrap the doily circle into a cone shape, leaving a small opening in the bottom for inserting trims. Turn under and crease the top overlap of the cone so the fold runs up the center front; secure with the hotmelt adhesive. Glue a piece of the garland ribbon up the center front.

Using 35" of the ⅛"-wide Dainty Double-faced Satin Ribbon, fold the length back and forth on itself every 5". Place two 5" lengths of the bead trim on top, then wrap florist's wire around the center. Glue the trim in the bottom of the cone.

For the hanger, glue the ends of the ¼"-wide red ribbon to the inside of the cone at the sides. Cut two 6" pieces of the ⅛"-wide ribbon. Tie each length into a small bow. Glue the bows to the outside of the cone, one on each side.

Carefully cut away the rest of the roses from the remaining rose-trimmed ribbon. Glue a rose in the center of each bow and one over the ends of the hanger on the inside of the cone. Glue the rest of the roses around the bottom of the cone.

Fill the cone with a bit of plastic foam. Glue wrapped candies to the top of the foam so they just peek out from the top of the ornament.

—Designed by Ellie Joos

MESH-RIBBON ORNAMENT

Shown on page 17 *and above.*
The ornament is 3" in diameter.

YOU WILL NEED:

⅔ yard of 2½"-wide red mesh ribbon
Glue gun and hotmelt adhesive
3"-diameter glass ornament
1 yard of ¼"-diameter red-and-gold cord
⅔ yard of 1½"-wide wire-edged gold mesh ribbon
10" length of ⅛"-wide metallic gold ribbon

INSTRUCTIONS

Cut the red mesh ribbon into two 10" lengths. In the center of one ribbon, pinch the long wired sides together and twist. Glue the twist to the bottom of the ornament.

Bring the ends of the ribbon up around the sides of the ornament, stretching the ribbon at the ornament's "equator" to measure 2½" wide. Pinch the cut ends together on each side of the ornament cap. Trim excess ribbon, if necessary. Glue the ribbon to the ornament at the top. Dab glue at the wired sides, if necessary. Repeat with the remaining piece of red mesh ribbon, gluing it across the first piece of ribbon.

Cut two 11" pieces of the cord. Glue the end of one cord to the side of the ornament cap. Wrap and glue the cord around the ornament, covering the seam (where the pieces

of mesh ribbon meet). Trim away any excess cord at the top. Repeat with the other length of cord, covering the remaining mesh ribbon seam. Wrap and glue a small piece of cord around the side of the ornament cap.

Cut the gold mesh ribbon in half. Tie each length into a bow. Set aside.

For the hanging loop, thread the metallic gold ribbon through the loop in the ornament cap, and knot the ends together. Glue the knot and the two bows to the top of the ornament.

—Designed by Ellie Joos

SHIMMERING SNOWFLAKE STOCKING

Shown on page 12 *and above.*
The stocking is 18" long.

YOU WILL NEED:

Chart opposite *and pattern on* page 38

For the stocking:
Tracing paper
⅝ yard of green velveteen fabric
Rotary cutter, rotary mat, and ruler
20×28" piece of thin fleece
⅔ yard of lining fabric; sewing threads
Mill Hill beads as follows: 1 package each of 00167 Christmas Green glass seed beads and 72020 Creme de Mint small bugle beads; 2 packages of 82020 Creme de Mint medium bugle beads

For the twisted-cord trims:
Kreinik #8 Fine Braid: 6¾ yards each of Silver 001 and Pearl 032
Kreinik Cord: 6¾ yards of Silver 001C
Kreinik Ombre: 13½ yards of Solid Pearl 3200
Cotton embroidery floss: 6¾ yards of white
Metallic embroidery floss: 6¾ yards of silver
Small clamp
For the cuff:
9×12" piece of 14-count Victorian Red Aida cloth
Embroidery hoop and needle
Cotton and metallic embroidery floss in the colors listed in the key *below*
Mill Hill seed beads in the colors listed in the key *below*
¼ yard of red taffeta fabric

INSTRUCTIONS

Trace the stocking pattern onto tracing paper. Add a ½" seam allowance all around the stocking. Cut out the completed pattern piece.

Piece the Stocking Front
From the green velveteen, cut thirteen 2×16" strips. With the right sides facing and using ¼" seam allowances, sew the long edges of the strips together to create a 16×20" rectangle.

Cut the pieced rectangle lengthwise into eight 2×20" strips. With the right sides facing and using ¼" seam allowances, sew the long edges of the

---

SHIMMERING SNOWFLAKE STOCKING

Anchor	DMC
☒	5283 Metallic Silver

BLENDED NEEDLE

002	⊟	000 White (2X) and 032 Kreinik Pearl blending filament (1X)

MILL HILL BEADS

◯	00479 White seed beads

Stitch count: 71 high x 110 wide
Finished design sizes:
14-count fabric – 5 x 7⅞ inches
16-count fabric – 4½ x 6⅞ inches
18-count fabric – 4 x 6⅛ inches

SHIMMERING SNOWFLAKE STOCKING CHART

Top

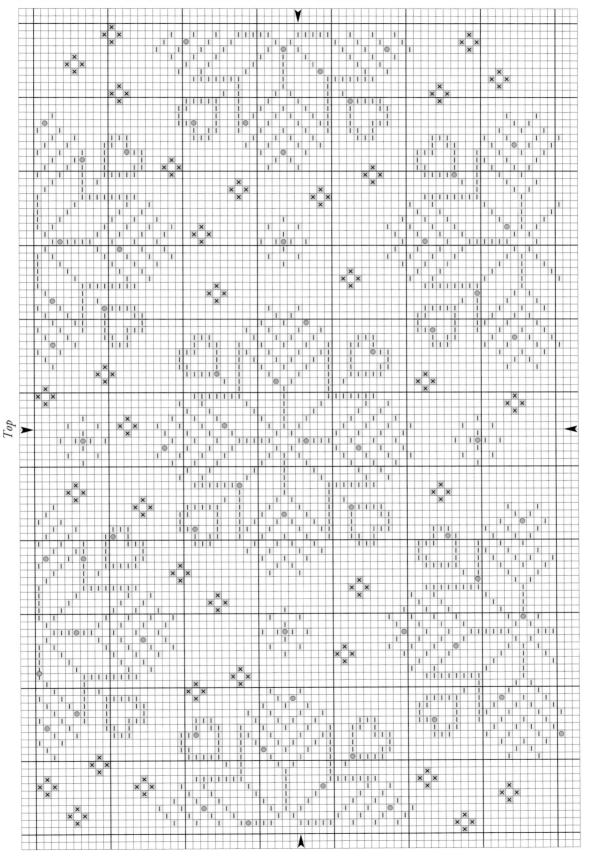

strips together, matching the seams, to create a 12½×20" rectangle.

Pin the stocking pattern to the pieced rectangle. Cut out the stocking front, adding a ½" seam allowance.

Bead and Assemble the Stocking

Cut one matching stocking back from the velveteen, two from the fleece, and two from the lining fabric. Baste

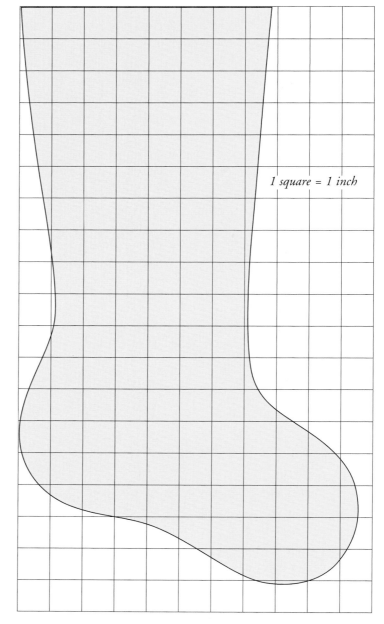

Beading Diagram

the fleece shapes to the wrong side of the pieced front and the stocking back. Using green sewing thread, stitch three Christmas Green glass seed beads to the center of each intersection on the pieced front (see the diagram *above*). Sew a small Creme de Mint bugle bead horizontally on each side of each bead trio and a medium Creme de Mint bugle bead above and below each bead trio.

With the right sides facing and using a ½" seam allowance, sew the stocking front to the back, leaving the top edge open. Clip the curves and turn the stocking right side out. Finger-press the seam.

Make the Twisted-Cord Trims

To make a 45"-length of twisted cord to trim the edge of the stocking, use 4-yard lengths of the threads (see the materials list), except use two 4-yard lengths of the Kreinik Ombre Solid Pearl. Hold all of the threads together as a single length. Knot one end of the length, and secure it to a table with the small clamp. Twist the other end of the length until the cord kinks back on itself. Fold the cord in half, letting the two halves twist together.

Hand-sew the twisted cord around the outside edge of the stocking.

To make about 30" of twisted cord for the stocking bow, cut a 2¾-yard length of each thread used for the twisted cord trim, except use two 2¾-yard lengths of the Kreinik Ombre Solid Pearl. Follow the directions for the stocking trim, knotting each end of the twisted cord. Tie the cord into a bow; tack the center to secure it. Set the bow aside.

Cross-Stitch the Cuff

Zigzag-stitch or overcast the edges of the Aida fabric to prevent fraying.

Find the center of the chart and the center of the fabric; begin stitching there. Use two plies of the silver metallic floss or two plies of the white embroidery floss blended with one strand of the Kreinik Pearl Blending Filament, as indicated on the key on *page 36*, to work the cross-stitches. When all cross-stitching is complete,

SNOWFLAKE AND VELVET STOCKINGS PATTERN

1 square = 1 inch

sew the pearl seed beads in place, as indicated on the chart.

Assemble the Cuff

Cut out the cross-stitched cuff front, adding a ½" seam allowance all around. Cut out a matching back and two lining pieces from red taffeta and two matching pieces of fleece.

Baste the fleece pieces to the wrong side of the cuff front and back. With the right sides facing, sew the cuff front and back together along the short sides. Press the seams open, then turn the cuff right side out.

With the right sides facing, sew the lining pieces together along the short sides. Press the seams open.

Slip the lining over the cuff so the right sides are facing. Sew together around the bottom edge. Trim the seam allowance, and turn the cuff right side out.

Finish the Stocking

Slip the lined cuff over the top of the stocking (with the cuff lining facing the right side of the stocking), matching the raw edges. Stitch the cuff to the stocking.

Cut a 2½×6" strip of red taffeta for the hanging loop. Fold the long raw edges of the strip to the center, and fold the strip in half. Stitch along the long edges. Fold the strip in half crosswise, forming a loop. Stitch the loop to the back edge of the cuff, matching raw edges.

Sew the stocking lining pieces together, leaving the top edge open and leaving an opening along one side for turning. Don't turn right side out.

Slip the stocking into the lining with the right sides facing and sew completely around the opening.

Turn the stocking right side out through the opening in the lining.

Slip-stitch the opening closed. Slip the lining inside the stocking.

Open out the cuff. Keeping the cuff free, topstitch through the stocking and the lining ¼" from the seam line around the top; turn down the cuff.

For the beaded edging, secure a thread at the bottom edge of the cuff at a side seam. Slip nine white seed beads on the thread, then count over five squares of the Aida cloth and take a tiny stitch, creating a beaded scallop. Continue in this manner all around the bottom edge of the cuff.

Tack the twisted-cord bow at the base of the hanging loop.

—Designed by Catherine Reurs

YULE LOG CRATE

Shown on page 11 *and above.*
The crate measures 10×12×18".

YOU WILL NEED:

10×12×18" wooden crate
Sandpaper and spray sanding sealer
Red spray paint
Precut wood shapes as follows: 7—2"-wide trees; 11—1"-wide and 6—2¼"-wide stars, and a set of 1½"-tall self-adhesive letters to spell "MERRY CHRISTMAS"
Green, red, and yellow acrylic paints
Paintbrush and wood glue
Spray acrylic varnish

INSTRUCTIONS

Sand the crate, and spray with sanding sealer. Allow to dry. Spray

the crate with two coats of the red paint, allowing to dry between coats.

Paint all of the precut wood trees green, half of the small stars red, and all of the large stars and the remaining small stars yellow. Allow to dry. Glue the small red stars to the center of the large yellow stars. Add a dot of green paint to the center of the red stars, using the handle end of the paintbrush. Glue the small yellow stars to the top of the trees. Add red dots to the trees for ornaments.

Referring to the photograph at *left,* glue the large stars across the top slat of the crate and the trees across the bottom slat. Glue the "MERRY CHRISTMAS" letters, centered, to the two middle slats. Let dry.

Spray the completed crate with varnish. Fill with wood and firestarter pinecones or with decorative Christmas packages.

—Designed by Margaret Sindelar

SILK LEAVES ORNAMENT

Shown on page 21.
The ornament is 3" in diameter.

YOU WILL NEED:

Offray Ribbons and Trims: 24 Medium Red Neva-Wilt Leaves (about 1¼×2¼") and 2 yards of ⅛"-wide Quasar Gold Ribbon
3"-diameter plastic-foam ball
Fine straight pins
Glue gun and hotmelt adhesive

INSTRUCTIONS

Note: The plastic-foam ball is covered with four rows of six leaves each. The first row adhered to the ball will be the bottom of the ornament.

For the first row of leaves, pin the tip of six leaves together at the bottom of the plastic-foam ball, overlapping the leaves. Glue the leaves to the ball.

For the second row, place the tip of one leaf 1" from the bottom of the ball, centering it over two overlapping leaves of the first row. Glue in place. Continue in this manner around the ball until the second row of six leaves is completed.

Glue the leaves for the third row 1" from the tips and between the leaves of the second row. Repeat for the fourth row, bringing the stem ends of the leaves together at the top of the ball and overlapping the leaves.

Cut the gold ribbon into one 12" strip and three 20" lengths.

For the hanging loop, fold the 12" piece of ribbon in half and tie an overhand knot about 4" from the fold. With the remaining ribbon, tie a bow with 1½" loops in the center of each ribbon length. Take the ends of each bow and tie a second same-size bow over the first. You now have three 4-loop bows.

Glue or pin the knot of the hanging loop and all three bows to the top of the ornament.

—*Designed by Ellie Joos*

SNAPPER CRACKER FAVORS

Shown on page 14 *and* below.
The favors are each 12" long.

YOU WILL NEED:

Heavy white paper
Transparent tape
Crepe paper or fabric
Snaps
Novelties: Jokes, fortunes, or riddles on strips of paper; small toys or other small prizes
Medium-weight cotton string
Ribbons, lace, raffia, or name tags

INSTRUCTIONS

Draw one 5×7" rectangle (for the center tube) and two 2¾×7" rectangles (one for each end tube) onto heavy white paper. Cut out the rectangles. Roll the short end of each piece to form tubes with equal diameters; secure along the edge with transparent tape.

Cut a 13×18" piece from the crepe paper or fabric. Lay the three tubes across the center of the crepe paper or fabric, leaving a gap of about ½" between each tube, and tape the crepe paper to the center roll. Roll the paper around the tubes; secure it with transparent tape. Place the snap through all three tubes and any novelties inside the center tube. Tie a length of string around the crepe paper at the gaps between the tubes, and tie tightly, cinching the crepe paper between the short and long tubes.

Tuck the ends of the crepe paper into the ends of the short tubes. Embellish the crackers by tying on lace, raffia, trims, ribbons, nametags, or other decorations.

—*Designed by Ann Blevins*

TRADITIONAL PLAID WREATH AND GARLAND

Shown on page 19 *and* above.
The wreath is 20" in diameter.

YOU WILL NEED:

Gold spray paint
30 eucalyptus branches
15 onion grass curls
12 yards of 6"-wide Offray MW Lassie Ribbon
6—4"-wide and 2—6½"-wide ornamental French horns
Thin wire
20"-diameter evergreen wreath
Glue gun and hotmelt adhesive
Fresh garland and cup hooks

INSTRUCTIONS

Spray the eucalyptus branches and onion grass curls with the gold spray paint. Set the sprayed pieces aside.

To make the wreath bow, cut a 2-yard length from the ribbon. Lay the first 15" of the ribbon flat on the working surface. Fold the ribbon back on itself for 15". Continue folding the ribbon back and forth 15" for the entire length. Wrap a piece of wire around the center, creating a four-loop bow. Trim the cut ends as desired. Wire the large French horn to the center of the bow, and wire the bow to the top of the wreath.

Cut a second 2-yard length from the ribbon to create the circle of "pouffs" around the wreath. Also cut six pieces of wire. At one end of the ribbon, pinch the wired sides together and wrap them with a piece of the wire. Repeat at the opposite end. Pinch and wire the ribbon at 14½" intervals. Tuck one end of the ribbon under the bow, wiring it to a branch of evergreen. Tuck and wire the other end under the bow on the opposite side. Tuck and secure the rest of the pinched ribbon sections around the wreath, creating five pouffs.

Glue the eucalyptus branches around the wreath, concentrating more branches at the top. Glue onion grass curls around the wreath. If desired, secure the ribbon bow to the wreath with dabs of hotmelt adhesive. Wire the small French horns to the evergreen branches, filling in any large open spaces on the wreath.

To hang the wreath, tie a bow in the center of the remaining length of ribbon, leaving about 18"-long tails. Securely wire the center of the bow, then tie or wire the ends of the tails to the back of the wreath, making sure the tails are of equal length so the wreath hangs straight.

For the garland, make hanging loops from wire, wiring them at even intervals along the back of the garland (we made three for our fireplace garland). Create a bow for each hanging loop position on the garland. Wire the bows to the front of the garland, and trim with eucalyptus, onion grass curls, and large French horns as directed for the wreath, above. Make pouffed lengths of ribbon to fit between the bows. Wire

the pouffs to the garland. Add small French horn ornaments, as desired.

To display the garland, screw cup hooks into the mantel, and slip the wire loops of the garland over the hooks. To avoid damaging your mantel, paint a piece of plywood to match your fireplace. Screw the cup hooks into the plywood, and use small clamps to hold the wood to the mantel. Style the garland and bows to conceal the clamps, adding extra greenery as necessary.

—Designed by Ellie Joos

WRAPPED-IN-RIBBONS PACKAGES

Shown on page 10 *and above.*

YOU WILL NEED:

For the large box:
8×8×3½" box with lid
Offray Ribbons and Cords: 1½ yards of 4"-wide and 1 yard of 2¼"-wide Wire-Edge Hartford Ribbon (plaid), ⅓ yard of ³⁄₁₆"-diameter Gold Morocco Cord, and ⅔ yard of 2"-wide Red Elan ribbon (mesh)
Glue gun and hotmelt adhesive
For the small box:
5×5×3" box with lid
Offray Ribbons and Cords: 1½ yards of 2¼"-wide Wire-Edge Hartford Ribbon (plaid), 1½ yards of ⅝"-wide Red Velvette Ribbon, 2 yards of ³⁄₁₆"-diameter Gold Morocco Cord, and 1 yard of ⅝"-wide Hunter Velvette ribbon
Glue gun and hotmelt adhesive

INSTRUCTIONS

Wrap the large box lid as follows. Cut the wide plaid ribbon into three 17" lengths. Cut the narrow plaid ribbon into two 17" lengths. Wrap two lengths of the wide ribbons, side by side, around the box lid. Glue the ends to the inside of the lid. Weave the remaining wide ribbon in the center and the two narrow ribbons, one on each side, through the ribbons on the lid. Wrap and secure the ribbons to the lid as before.

Cut the gold cord in half. Referring to the photograph on *page 10*, tie one piece of cord around each of the narrow plaid ribbons on top of the lid. Hide the knots beneath the ribbons. Wrap the mesh ribbon around the wide plaid ribbon on the top of the lid and tie into a bow.

Wrap the small box lid as follows. Cut the ribbons and cord into four 13" lengths. (Save the excess gold cord for the package bow.) Weave the four plaid ribbons on the top of the box lid. (Don't worry about the space between the ribbons; it will be covered later with the velvet ribbons.) Wrap the ribbons around the lid, and glue the ends to the inside of the lid. Also glue the ribbons to the lid at the corners.

Weave two of the velvet ribbons over the plaid ribbons to cover the open spaces. Wrap and glue as for the plaid ribbons. Weave, wrap, and glue gold cords next to these velvet ribbons. Referring to the photograph on *page 10*, wrap the remaining two velvet ribbons and cords, parallel to the first, around the lid. Glue the ribbons to the inside of the lid. Fashion a four-loop bow from the green velvet ribbon. Tie the remaining gold cord into a bow. Glue the two bows together to the top of the box lid.

—Designed by Ellie Joos

COUNTRY
🌿 COLLECTION 🌿

*O*ur celebration of a country Christmas comes complete with such charming traditional crafts as a quilt to sew, *opposite,* a Nativity and floorcloth to paint, an old-fashioned feather tree to create, cards to decorate, a doll and miniature tree skirt to sew, a pillow to cross-stitch, and much more. Simple Santas and snowmen also offer seasonal motifs and rustic accents you'll treasure for many Christmases to come.

Instructions begin on page 54.

43

COZY LOG CABIN QUILT

Your Christmas guests will love
to snuggle up in this soft
flannel quilt made in traditional
reds and greens with a country flair.
The design is based on a traditional
log cabin block motif, with black
buttons sewn to the center of each
block for the perfect finishing touch.
Instructions are on page 54.

OLD-FASHIONED FEATHER TREE

Feather trees of yesteryear were traditionally fashioned from goose
feathers, which were painstakingly crafted by wrapping the feathers
one by one onto the branches of a tree form. You'll be amazed how
quickly you can fashion your own authentic-looking feather tree using
artificial greenery, dried rosehips, a dowel, and florist's tape.
Instructions are on page 56.

QUILTED KRIS KRINGLE

St. Nick has never looked more endearing than in this
folk art doll rendition depicting him in a cozy patchwork coat and red
linen trousers. His easy-to-draw face and wavy, thick yarn hair and beard also
contribute to his quaint character. Instructions are on page 56.

JOLLY OLD NICK PILLOW

Santas never go out of style, and our designers love to create
fresh country looks to brighten your holiday decorating. Cross-stitch
this Santa picture on an Aida cloth pillow front and add colorful buttons
to define the running-stitch border. Instructions are on page 60.

$\mathcal{S}$ILENT NIGHT NATIVITY

Our Nativity combines the joys of woodcrafting and painting.
We'll show you how to scrollsaw the shapes and paint the patterns to create
this traditional motif with a wonderfully original, whimsical country style.
Instructions are on page 63.

$\mathcal{C}$IRCLE OF SANTAS
MINI TREE SKIRT

Part of the fun at Christmas is making gifts for your friends and family. Our easy
mini tree skirt makes a great gift anyone would love, and is the perfect size for a tabletop tree.
Simply use crayons and an outline-stitch to complete the Santa and tree pattern,
then sew the skirt form, and bind the edges with coordinating fabric. Instructions are on page 63.

JOLLY SNOWMAN ORNAMENT

A dried gourd springs to life as a smiling hand-painted snowman for your country Christmas decorating. The dimensions of the gourd suggest the design, with the stem forming the snowman's jaunty top hat and the base shaping his roly-poly body. Instructions are on page 69.

HOMESPUN HOLIDAY GREETINGS

Form festive holiday greeting cards using textured papers layered for a background and cut into snowman and angel shapes. Add strips of homespun fabric and hand-inked facial details and lettering to customize your cards. Instructions are on page 64.

Heavenly Snowman Angel

Many who enjoy woodcrafts and painting turn to whimsical country designs when making crafts for their holiday decorating. We offer this easy to scrollsaw and simple to paint heavenly snowman that sports a pair of angel wings and tops his holiday tree with a Christmas star. Instructions are on page 73.

Snowmen Friends Floorcloth

Snowman motifs offer country appeal during the Christmas season—and they are fun to display throughout the winter around your hearth. Our designer painted a repeat-motif snowman border and a falling snowflakes pattern on this canvas floorcloth that brightens a brick fireplace. Instructions are on page 70.

COZY LOG CABIN QUILT

Shown on pages 42, 44, and below.
The finished quilt is 63×89". Each
finished block is 13" square.

YOU WILL NEED:

⅝ yard of solid black fabric for blocks and
  inner border

1 yard of black-and-white check print for
  blocks and binding

6—⅓-yard pieces each of assorted red and
  green flannel prints for blocks

2⅜ yards of green flannel for outer border

5⅜ yards of backing fabric

69×95" piece of quilt batting

24—1⅛"-diameter black shank buttons

Rotary cutter, quilting ruler, and cutting mat

90° right triangle

Note: *The fabric quantities specified in*
the materials list are for 44/45"-wide,
100% cotton fabrics. All measurements
include a ¼" seam allowance unless
otherwise stated.

INSTRUCTIONS

Cut the Fabrics

Note: *To make the best use of your*
fabrics, cut the pieces in the order that
follows. (Project designer Margaret
Sindelar used strips of the same fabric
consecutively to make each block.)

From the solid black, cut:
• 48—2½" squares for block centers
• 7—1½×42" strips for inner border

From the black-and-white check
print, cut:
• 48—2½" squares for block centers
• 8—2½×42" strips for binding

From assorted red flannel prints, cut:
• 24—2×4½" strips for position 1
• 24—2×6" strips for position 2
• 24—2×7½" strips for position 5
• 24—2×9" strips for position 6
• 24—2×10½" strips for position 9
• 24—2×12" strips for position 10

From the assorted green flannel
prints, cut:
• 24—2×6" strips for position 3
• 24—2×7½" strips for position 4
• 24—2×9" strips for position 7
• 24—2×10½" strips for position 8
• 24—2×12" strips for position 11
• 24—2×13½" strips for position 12

From the green flannel, cut:
• 2—5×83" outer border strips
• 2—5×75" outer border strips

Assemble the Log Cabin Blocks

Diagram 1

Lay out two solid black and two
black-and-white check print 2½"
squares in two rows (see Diagram 1,
above). Sew together the squares in
each row. Press the seam allowances
toward the solid black squares.

Join the rows to make a Four-Patch
unit. Press the seam allowance in one
direction. The pieced Four-Patch unit
should measure 4½" square, including
the seam allowances. Repeat to make
a total of 24 Four-Patch units.

With the right sides together, align a
red flannel print position 1 strip with
the top edge of a Four-Patch unit (see
Diagram 2, *opposite*). Press the seam
allowance toward the red strip.
Referring to Diagram 3, *opposite*, sew
a red flannel print position 2 strip to

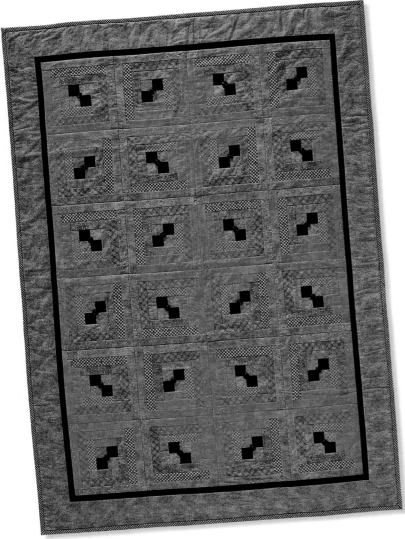

Diagram 2   *Diagram 3*

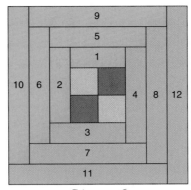

Diagram 6

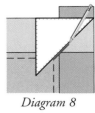

Diagram 8

the left edge of the Four-Patch unit. Press and trim the strip as before.

Referring to Diagram 4, *below,* add a green print position 3 strip to the bottom edge of the Four-Patch unit. Press and trim the strip as before. Referring to Diagram 5, *below,* add a green print position 4 strip to the right edge of the Four-Patch unit. Press and trim.

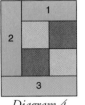

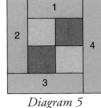

Diagram 4   *Diagram 5*

Continue sewing strips to the block center in a counterclockwise direction, following the numerical sequence in Diagram 6, *above right,* to complete one Log Cabin block. Always press seam allowances toward the outside of the block. The pieced block should measure 13½" square, including seam allowances. Repeat to make a total of 24 blocks.

Assemble the Quilt Top

Referring to the photograph, *opposite,* lay out the blocks in six rows of four blocks each as shown. Sew together the blocks in each row. Press the seam allowances in each row in one direction, alternating the direction with each row. Sew together the rows to complete the pieced quilt top. Press the seam allowances in one direction. The pieced quilt top should measure 52½×78½", including the seam allowances.

Add the Borders

Cut and piece the solid black 1½×42" strips into the following:

- 2—1½×78½" inner border strips
- 2—1½×54½" inner border strips

Sew one solid black 1½×78½" inner border strip to each side edge of the pieced top. Then add one black print 1½×54½" inner border strip to the top edge of the pieced top and one to the bottom edge. Press all seam allowances toward the black print border. With right sides together and midpoints aligned, pin the green print 5×83" outer border strip to an edge of the pieced quilt center; allow the excess border fabric to extend beyond the edges. Sew together, beginning and ending the seam ¼" from the corners (see Diagram 7, *below*).

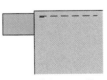

Diagram 7

Repeat with the remaining green print 5×83"and 5×75" outer border strips. Press the seam allowance toward the border strips.

Miter the outer border corners. To miter a corner, overlap adjacent border strips (see Diagram 8, *above right*). Align the edge of a 90° right triangle with the raw edge of the

border strip on top so the long edge of the triangle intersects the seam in the corner. With a pencil, draw along the edge of the triangle from the seam out to the raw edge. Repeat for the remaining three border corners.

With the right sides together, match the marked lines and pin the pieces together (see Diagram 9, *below*).

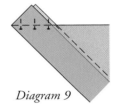

Diagram 9

Beginning with a backstitch at the inside corner, stitch exactly on the marked lines to the raw edges of the border strips. Check the right side of the corner to see that it lays flat. Then trim the excess fabric, leaving a ¼" seam allowance. Press the seam open.

Complete the Quilt

Cut and piece the backing fabric to measure at least 3" bigger on all sides than the quilt top. Press the seam allowances open. With the wrong sides together, layer the quilt top and the backing fabric with the piece of batting in between the layers. Baste the layers. Machine- or hand-quilt as desired. Piece the black-and-white check print 2½×42" strips to make one long continuous binding; bind the quilt. Hand-sew a black shank button to the center of each block using coordinated sewing thread.

—Designed by Margaret Sindelar

OLD-FASHIONED FEATHER TREE

Shown on page 45.

YOU WILL NEED:

Artificial greenery garland
Wire clippers
Small handsaw
$3/8$"- and 1"-diameter dowels
Roll of green florist's tape
Drill and $3/8$" and 1" drill bits
$3\frac{1}{4} \times 3\frac{1}{4} \times 6$" wooden finial
5 to 7 metal washers and wood glue
Sponge brush and red acrylic paint
Glue gun and hotmelt adhesive
Dried rosehips

INSTRUCTIONS

Untwist the garland wires to release the branches. With wire clippers, cut 60 lengths of the garland, each measuring 11" long. Saw the $3/8$"-diameter dowel 25" long; saw a 1"-length from the 1"-diameter dowel.

Use six lengths of garland for each row of branches. Starting with the bottom row, lay six branches flat against and around the long dowel, placing the bottom ends of the branches 2" from the end of the dowel. Tightly wrap florist's tape around the branch ends for $2\frac{1}{2}$". Fold the branches down. For the next row, lay six branches around the dowel in the same manner; the ends of the branches should just meet the folded-down row of branches. Wrap as before. Continue adding rows in this manner to fill the dowel. Trim the branch rows in graduating lengths.

Drill a 1"-diameter hole in the bottom of the finial and a $3/8$"-diameter hole in the top, each 2" deep. Insert metal washers in the bottom hole to add weight and stability; secure the 1"-long dowel into the bottom hole with wood glue.

Let dry. Paint the finial with a sponge brush and red acrylic paint. Let dry. Insert the tree trunk into the top of the finial; secure it with wood glue. Allow to dry. Glue dried rosehips to the ends of the branches.

—*Designed by Ann Blevins*

QUILTED KRIS KRINGLE

Shown on page 46 *and* opposite. *The finished doll is 20" tall.*

YOU WILL NEED:

Patterns on pages 58 *and* 59

Tracing paper
$1/8$ yard of muslin
$1/4$ yard of black cotton
Rotary cutter, acrylic ruler, and cutting mat
Polyester fiberfill and matching sewing thread
$1/2$ yard of red plaid flannel
$1/2$ yard of red linen
$1/2$-yard piece of an old quilt
$1/2$ yard of monk's cloth
$1/2$ yard of cream or white wool
8"-diameter embroidery hoop and rug hook
Tan dye and spray bottle
Brown embroidery floss and jute twine
Black ultra-fine tip permanent marking pen
1 ounce of Thick & Thin Natural material
Glue gun and hotmelt adhesive
12" twig for Santa's staff

INSTRUCTIONS

Note: *All measurements include a $1/4$" seam allowance unless otherwise noted. The doll body, coat, and hat are sewn wrong sides together with the seams on the outside.*

Trace the pattern pieces onto tracing paper and cut out.

Make the Santa Body

Fold the muslin fabric in half with the right sides facing. Draw around the body pattern on the wrong side of the fabric. Fold the black cotton fabric in half with right sides facing.

Draw around the arms and legs patterns on the wrong side of the fabric. Cut out the pieces.

With the right sides together, sew around the arms and legs, leaving the ends open. Clip the curves and turn right side out. Firmly stuff to the lines shown on the pattern and sew across.

With wrong sides facing, pin the body pieces together. Begin sewing at the bottom right-side edge of the body, inserting the arms between the pattern dots as you go. Don't sew across the bottom of the body or turn. Firmly stuff the body, making sure to fill the neck and head well. Insert the legs into the body opening, and sew across the body bottom.

Make the Clothes

Draw around the shirt pattern on the wrong side of the plaid flannel. With right sides together, sew the underarms and side seams. Do not sew the neck opening. Clip and turn.

Fold the red linen in half with right sides facing. Draw around the pants pattern on the wrong side of the fabric; cut out. With the right sides together, sew the side and inside seams, leaving the top and bottom open. Clip and turn.

Fold the quilt piece in half with the right sides facing. Draw around the coat and hat patterns on the wrong side of the fabric and cut out.

With the wrong sides together, sew the side and underarms of the coat. Clip the seams. Cut the front opening as shown on the pattern. With the wrong sides together, sew the side seam of the hat, leaving the top and bottom open.

Hook the Trim

Draw the hat- and cuff-trim patterns and a 1×50" rectangle for the coat

trim on the monk's cloth, leaving at least 1" between them; do not cut out. Stitch around the drawn shapes using a ¼" seam allowance and a small zigzag stitch. Center the cloth in an 8" embroidery hoop.

Using scissors or a rotary cutter, an acrylic quilter's ruler, and a self-healing cutting mat, cut the cream or white wool into ¼"-wide strips along the straight grain of the fabric to make the hooking strips.

To hook the design, follow the diagrams, *right.* (Right-handed people work best from top to bottom or right to left.) Hold a woolen strip loosely between the thumb and forefinger of your left hand and beneath the monk's cloth. Hold the

Diagram 1

Diagram 2

rug hook in your right hand with the hook up. Insert the hook through the mesh. The shaft of the hook should touch your left forefinger and slide under the wool strip (see Diagram 1,

below left). Pull the end of the strip to the top side, leaving a ½" tail (see Diagram 2, *below left).* All of the ends will be pulled up to the top and cut off later even with the hooked loops. Use your thumbnail underneath the fabric as a guide for placing the loops. Keep the underneath strip smooth against the cloth.

For the first loop, push the hook into a second or third mesh, and slide the hook under the strip. ***Note:*** *Always maneuver the hook at a 45° angle. If you hold the hook too upright, you may catch the foundation threads in the hook when you pull the strip through to the top of the fabric.*

Pull the loop to the top, and roll it back toward the tail. The loop should be pulled up about as high as it is wide. At the end of the strip, pull the tail through to the top. Start the next strip in the hole where the previous tail ended. (The ends will share the same hole.) Work strips in straight lines. When the area is hooked, trim the tails even with the loops.

Cut out the trim, cutting ⅛" outside the zigzag stitches to stabilize the monk's cloth. Turn the raw edges under ¼" and whipstitch the cuffs and hat trims in place.

For the coat trim, begin at the center back of the coat with one end of the trim. Whipstitch the trim to the coat, going around the edges and meeting the ends at the back.

Mix 1 part tan dye to 12 parts water in a spray bottle. Spritz the trim with the dye mixture.

Felt the trim while it's still damp. To felt, press with a steam iron on a cotton setting. Hang to dry.

Embellish the Doll

Lace the boots with six strands of brown embroidery floss and a large

QUILTED KRIS KRINGLE PATTERNS

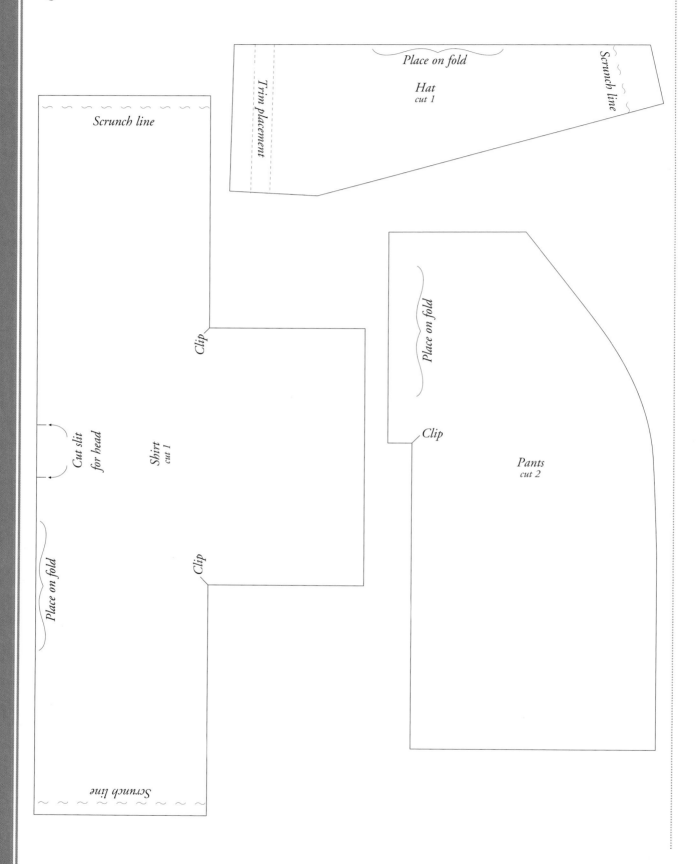

Place on fold

Hat
cut 1

Scrunch line

Trim placement

Scrunch line

Clip

Cut slit
for head

Shirt
cut 1

Clip

Place on fold

Clip

Pants
cut 2

Place on fold

Place on fold

Scrunch line

QUILTED KRIS KRINGLE PATTERNS

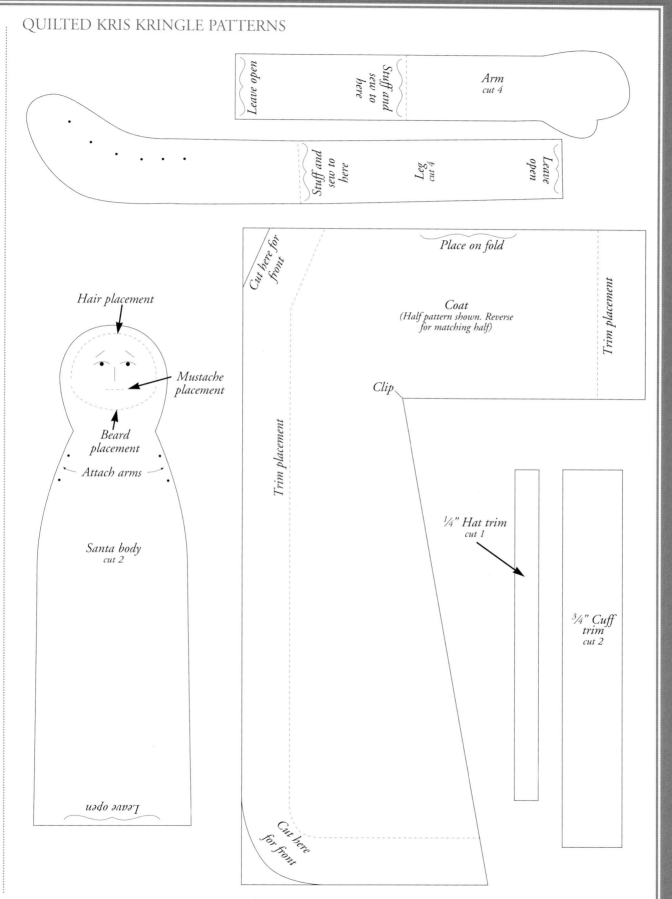

Leave open

Stuff and sew to here

Arm
cut 4

Stuff and sew to here

Leg
cut 4

Leave open

Cut here for front

Place on fold

Coat
(Half pattern shown. Reverse for matching half)

Trim placement

Clip

Trim placement

Hair placement

Mustache placement

Beard placement

Attach arms

Santa body
cut 2

Leave open

Cut here for front

¼" Hat trim
cut 1

¾" Cuff trim
cut 2

cross-stitch, following the lacing dots on the pattern. Knot and leave the ends loose. Place the shirt over Santa's head. Put the arms in the sleeves, scrunch the fabric around each wrist, and tie with jute. Put on his pants, tuck in the shirt, and tie the waist with a 12"-long piece of jute. Scrunch the fabric around each leg, and tie it with a 6" piece of jute.

Cut several 10"-long pieces of Thick and Thin Natural material for the strands of the beard and mustache. Beginning at the bottom of Santa's face, fold the strands in half, and whipstitch the fold onto the face. Refer to the placement lines on the pattern. Cut 2"-long pieces of Thick and Thin Natural material for strands of hair. Sew the strands on as indicated by the mustache and hair placement on the pattern.

Draw the eyes and nose with the permanent marking pen, as shown on the pattern. Whipstitch the hat to the head, covering the hairline. Tie the tip of the hat with a 6" piece of jute. Put on Santa's coat. Glue the staff to the inside of his hand.

—Designed by Leslie Beck of Fiber Mosaics

JOLLY OLD NICK PILLOW

Shown on page 47 and below.
The pillow measures 18" square. The finished stitchery measures 6½×8½".

YOU WILL NEED:

Chart opposite

11×13" piece of 18-count Slate/Rue Green Aida cloth

Cotton embroidery floss in the colors listed in the key, *below right*

Size 26 tapestry needle and embroidery hoop

Pencil; sewing thread to match the Aida cloth

18"-square red purchased pillow or fabric and fiberfill to make your own pillow

8 assorted red, green, ecru, and brown buttons, ranging in size from ½" in diameter to 1" in diameter

INSTRUCTIONS

Zigzag-stitch or overcast the edges of the fabric to prevent fraying.

Find the center of the chart and the fabric; begin stitching there. Work the cross-stitches using two plies of the embroidery floss. Work the backstitches using one ply of the embroidery floss.

Press the completed stitchery from the back side with a warm iron.

Lay the stitched piece facedown,

and lightly draw a line with a pencil about 1⅝" from the top and the sides of the Dark Garnet oval and 2¼" from the bottom edge. Using sewing thread to match the Aida cloth, machine-stitch along the drawn pencil line. Trim the fabric approximately four squares outside the stitched line on all sides.

Fray the edges of the fabric by pulling out the fabric threads along each side. The sewn line will help prevent further raveling.

Center the design on the purchased pillow. Thread a long sewing needle with six plies of the Dark Garnet embroidery floss. Stitch a running stitch through the cross-stitch fabric and the pillow, about nine squares inside the frayed edge; make the running stitches uneven.

Using six plies of embroidery floss, attach one to three buttons at each corner of the cross-stitch fabric.

—Designed by Pamela Kellogg

JOLLY OLD NICK PILLOW

Anchor		DMC	
387	⊡		Ecru
9046	♡	321	Christmas red
683	●	500	Blue-green
046	★	666	Red
1021	⊞	761	Salmon
045	♥	814	Dark garnet
1005	◙	816	Light garnet
4146	╱	950	Light rose-beige
189	⊞	991	Aquamarine
905	◆	3021	Deep brown-gray
899	⫴	3023	Light brown-gray
391	⊠	3033	Mocha
1008	△	3773	Medium rose-beige

BACKSTITCH (1X)

152	╱	939	Navy – holly leaves
189	╱	991	Aquamarine – stripes behind Santa
905	╱	3021	Deep brown-gray – all other stitches

FRENCH KNOT

905	○	3021	Deep brown-gray – holly berries (1X wrapped once)

Stitch count: 92 high x 62 wide
Finished design sizes:
18-count fabric – 5⅛ x 3½ inches
16-count fabric – 5¾ x 3⅞ inches
14-count fabric – 6½ x 4½ inches

JOLLY OLD NICK
PILLOW CHART

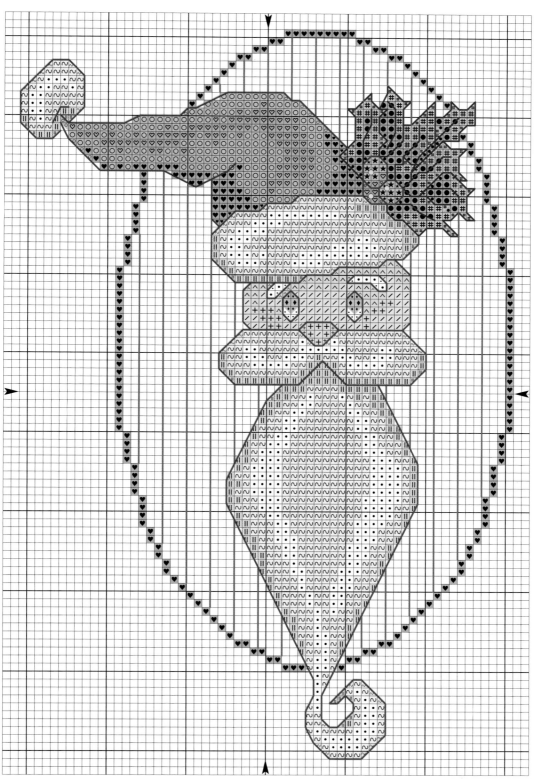

SILENT NIGHT
NATIVITY PATTERNS

SILENT NIGHT NATIVITY
Shown on page 48.

YOU WILL NEED:
Patterns on page 62

Tracing paper and transfer paper
12×12×1" pine
Scrollsaw with #5R blade
100- and 150-grit sandpaper
Tack cloth and wood sealer
Plaid FolkArt Acrylic paint: Apple Spice 951 (AS), Barn Wood 936 (BA), Buckskin Brown 418 (KB), Camel 953 (CA), Clay Bisque 601 (CL), Coffee Bean 940 (CB), Dapple Gray 937 (DG), English Mustard 959 (EM), Gray Mist 702 (GR), Indigo 908 (IN), Licorice 938 (LI), Mushroom 472 (MR), Parchment 450 (PH), Plum Pudding 934 (PN), Settler's Blue 607 (SE), and Skintone 949 (SK)
Plaid FolkArt Artist's Pigment paint: Turner's Yellow 679 (TY)
Loew-Cornell paintbrushes: Series 7300 #6 and #10 shaders, series 7000 rounds #0 and #2/0, and series 7350 liner #10/0
Plaid FolkArt Satin Varnish
Plaid FolkArt Apple Butter Brown Antiquing Medium

INSTRUCTIONS
Trace and transfer the outlines of the figure patterns onto 1" pine (actual thickness: ¾").

Cut out the shapes with a scrollsaw, using a #5R blade. Sand all surfaces with 100- and then 150-grit sandpaper, and remove the sanding dust with a tack cloth.

Apply wood sealer to all surfaces, and let the sealer dry. Sand again with 150-grit sandpaper, and wipe clean with a tack cloth.

Note: *Once each piece is painted, add the remaining outlines and details with thinned LI, as shown in the photographs, page 48. Instructions for "thinned" paint refer to paint with an ink consistency.*

Mary: Base-coat the shoulders to the top of the head PH. Paint the halo TY. Brush-float a PH border around the halo. Paint the face SK. Paint cheeks thinned AS, hair CB, dress SE, sleeve trim MR, and the hand SK.

Child: Base-coat the child PH and the halo TY. Float a PH border around the halo. Paint the face SK. Paint cheeks with a wash of AS.

Joseph: Base-coat the robe PN, the head covering MR, and the face, neck, and hands SK. Paint the trim and band on the head covering IN. Paint the zigzag trim on the robe MR and the belt sash KB.

Base-coat Joseph's lamb CL. Add swirls of DG and then GR for the lamb's wool. Paint the lamb's head and legs LI.

Donkey: Base-coat the donkey BA. Paint the muzzle and ankles PH. Paint the inside of his ears a wash of AS. Paint the mane, tail, and hooves LI. Use thinned PH to paint the details on the mane and tail.

Camel: Base-coat the camel CA. Add LI to the hooves and tail. Detail the tail PH.

Sheep: Base-coat the sheep CL. Add swirls of DG and then GR for the sheep's wool. Paint the head, legs, and ears LI. Use thinned GR to paint the eye.

Cow: Base-coat the cow CB. Paint spots KB and hooves and eyes LI.

Hen: Base-coat the hen LI, and add PH spots. Paint the eye and beak EM, the pupil LI, and the comb and waddle AS.

Apply one coat of varnish to each piece. Let dry. Using a soft cloth, apply antiquing medium and wipe off for the desired shade. Let dry.

Finish the pieces with a second coat of varnish. Allow to dry.

—*Designed by Susan Fouts-Kline*

CIRCLE OF SANTAS MINI TREE SKIRT
Shown on page 49 *and above.*
The tree skirt is 12" in diameter.

YOU WILL NEED:
Pattern on page 68

½ yard of tan fabric
¼ yard of plaid fabric
½ yard of cotton batting
Compass and straight edge
Freezer paper
Tracing paper and masking tape
White paper towels
Black ultra-fine tip permanent marking pen
Crayola™ crayons: Red, green, black, white, gold, apricot or flesh, and tan
Tapestry needle and black embroidery floss

INSTRUCTIONS
Fold the tan fabric in half; place the batting in between the layers and pin together. Using a compass, draw a 12"-diameter circle on the fabric. Using the same center point, draw a 1⅜"-diameter circle inside the large circle. Using a straight edge, draw a wedge from the outside circle to the inner circle that is ¼"-wide at the outer circle. Through all layers, cut out the large circle, wedge, and center circle. Press the freezer paper onto the back of one of the fabric circles for

stability. Trace the pattern onto tracing paper and cut it out.

Center the fabric circle with the freezer paper backing over the pattern; tape it to a light table or a large window. Trace the pattern with the marking pen, moving the pattern around the fabric circle to evenly trace the pattern around the circle.

Color the fabric inside the pattern lines with the crayons. ***Note:*** *Keep the crayons sharp as you work. The colors will fade, so select a crayon shade darker than the one you want for your finished project. White crayon will fade entirely, so use it only after heat setting.* Fill in the design heavily with crayons to the desired intensity, and shade with a lighter hue. Remove the freezer paper when coloring is completed.

Place several layers of paper towels on an ironing board. Place the colored design face down on the towels. Cover the design with more paper towels, and use a dry iron on a cotton setting to press it. Do not slide the iron. The wax will melt into the towels. After pressing once, replace the used towels with fresh ones. Repeat until the design is free of wax. If the color fades, let the fabric cool, reapply the colors, and heat-set again. Color Santa's beard and mustache white. Using two plies of black floss, backstitch the designs and make French knots for Santa's eyes.

With wrong sides together, layer the top and backing with the batting in between. Beginning at the center, smooth out the wrinkles; pin. Using a ⅜" seam allowance, sew around the outside edge of the tree skirt. Use 2"-wide bias strips of plaid binding fabric to bind the edges.

—Designed by Leslie Beck of Fiber Mosaics

HOMESPUN HOLIDAY GREETINGS

Shown on pages 50 *and* 51 *and* above.

YOU WILL NEED:

Patterns on pages 65–67

For each card:
5×7" craft card with envelope
Deckle-edge scissors
Teflon™ pressing sheet and small paintbrush
Double-stick tape or rubber cement
For the angel cards:
1 sheet *each* of cream and green corrugated paper
1 sheet of olive green card stock
¼ yard of fusible appliqué film
Cotton fabric scraps in plaids, red, greens, browns, golds, peach, and ecru
Acrylic paint in black and brown
Cosmetic sponge
Permanent Pigma pens: Black, brown, and red
Brown rubber stamp ink pad
Cream powder blush and cotton swab
Hole punch
For the snowmen cards:
2 sheets of dark-red card stock
2 sheets of black textured paper
½ yard *each* of fusible appliqué film and fusible woven interfacing
Cotton fabric scraps: White, red, green, gold
Acrylic paint in black and orange
Large needle; 12" of light-gauge gold wire
Silver-metallic marker

INSTRUCTIONS

For the angel cards: Using deckle-edge scissors, trim the cream corrugated paper to 4½×6½", the green

corrugated paper to 4×5¼", and the olive green card stock to 4×6".

For the snowmen cards: Using deckle-edge scissors, trim the dark-red card stock to 4½×6½" and the black textured paper to 4×6".

Fuse a piece of the woven fusible interfacing to the back of the white cotton fabric to prevent the black background from showing through.

Trace the patterns for the angel and snowmen cards onto the appliqué film. Cut out the pieces, leaving a ⅛" margin around each piece.

Referring to the photographs on *pages 50* and *51,* fuse the appliqué film pieces to the desired fabrics; cut out the designs on the drawn lines. Remove the paper backings. For each card, layer the pieces on a Teflon pressing sheet before fusing them to the background. Refer to the placement diagrams, *opposite,* and on *pages 66* and *67,* for positioning the designs. Fuse the designs in place.

For the angel cards: Paint dots inside the angel's crown points.

Paint the eyes with black or brown dots using the handle end of a small paintbrush. Ink the eye shape, eyebrows, nose, lips, freckles, the lettering, and the stitching lines with the Pigma pens.

Tap the cosmetic sponge on the brown ink pad, blot on a paper towel, and shade the olive green card stock along the edges.

Write "Peace" on the flying angel's skirt with the brown pen.

Using the double-stick tape or rubber cement, layer the corrugated paper on the card stock.

For the standing angel card, center and punch two holes on the top of the card for the bow. Cut a 1×8" strip from a scrap of fabric.

To thread the card, begin at the

HOMESPUN HOLIDAY
GREETINGS PATTERNS

Placement Diagram

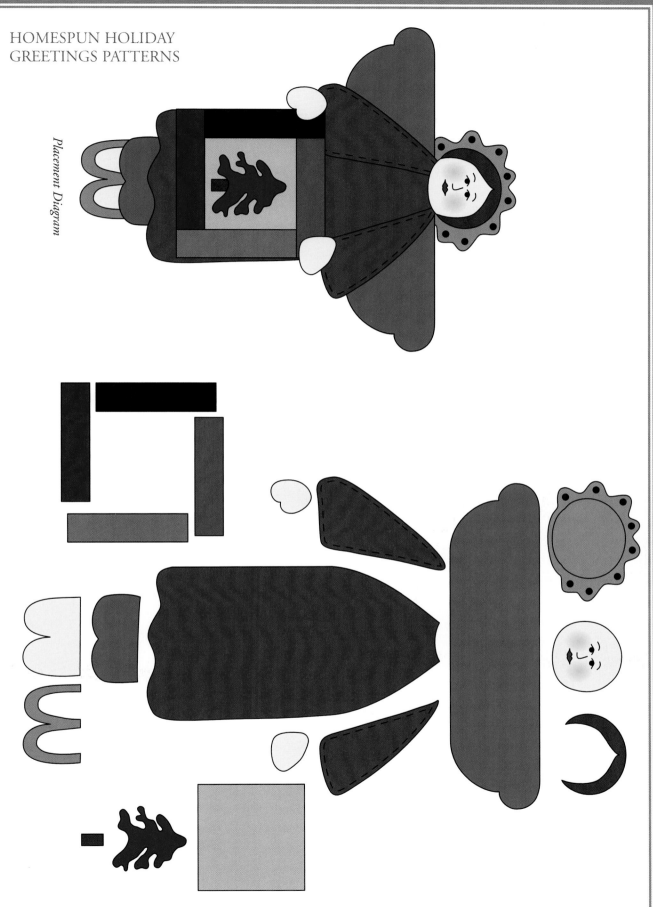

HOMESPUN HOLIDAY
GREETINGS PATTERNS

Placement Diagram

Placement Diagram

HOMESPUN HOLIDAY
GREETINGS PATTERNS

Placement Diagram

CIRCLE OF SANTAS
MINI TREE SKIRT PATTERN

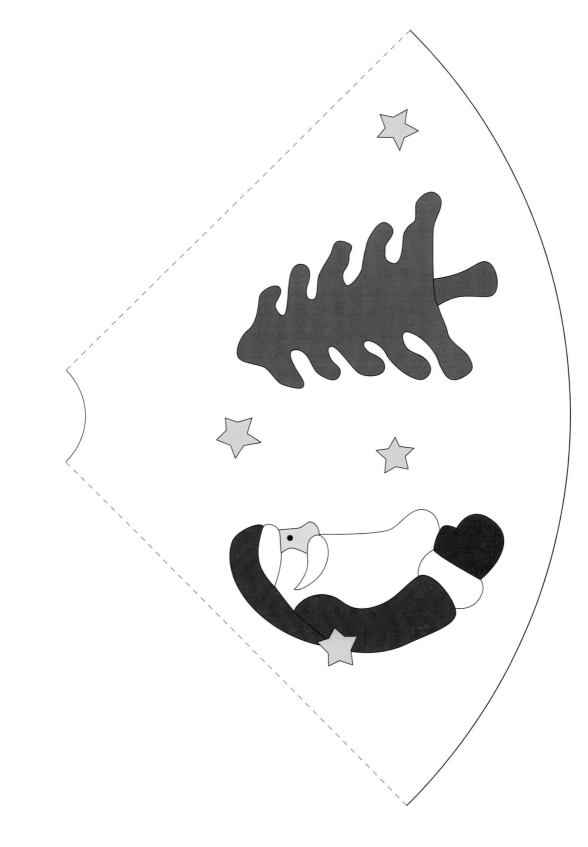

front and thread the fabric ends through each hole. Crisscross the ends at the back of the card, then thread the fabric ends through the opposite holes to the front of card. Pull the ends snug, and then trim them to size.

Apply cream powder blush with a cotton swab to color the angel cheeks for both cards.

For the snowmen cards: Paint the eyes and coal buttons with black dots using the handle end of a small paintbrush. Paint the fringe on the scarf and mittens black. Paint the carrot nose orange.

To make the star banner for the single snowman, use a large needle to poke one hole in each mitten and two holes in each star. Wrap the gold wire around a toothpick to curl it. Thread the wire through the holes, beginning and ending with each mitten. Leave a ½" tail of the twisted wire resting in each mitten.

Dot the black background using the silver-metallic marker.

Using the double-stick tape or rubber cement, layer the card stock and the textured paper pieces as shown in the photographs on *pages 50* and *51*.

—Designed by Leslie Beck of
Fiber Mosaics

JOLLY SNOWMAN ORNAMENT
Shown on page 51.

YOU WILL NEED:

Dried, clean gourd (see instructions, right)
Delta Ceramcoat Acrylic paint: Adobe 2046 (AO), Black 2506, Quaker Gray 2057 (QG), and White 2505
Paintbrushes: Loew Cornell white nylon series 797, size 6 and a small round fabric scrubber

1 tube orange Fanci Quick Design compound and decorating tip
Black posterboard and X-ACTO knife
Drill and drill bits
Spray matte sealer
MUD oil-based antiquing medium
Gloss varnish
Scrap of fabric
Small pieces of artificial greenery garland and berries
Glue gun and hotmelt adhesive
Goop glue
Raffia and 2 long tree twigs

INSTRUCTIONS

The gourd must be clean and thoroughly dry before it can be painted. See the instructions for preparing gourds, right. Base-coat the gourd White.

For the nose, screw the decorating tip onto the tube of orange compound; squeeze and pull out the compound, forming a pointed pile. Allow to dry for several days.

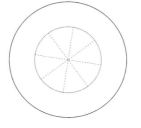

Diagram 1: Hat

Measure the circumference of the top of the gourd to determine the hat size. With a pencil, draw a circle at the determined circumference onto black posterboard. Draw a second circle outside the first circle that is ½" larger in circumference. Using an X-ACTO knife, cut slashes inside the smaller circle, referring to Diagram 1, *above*. Pull the hat over the top of the gourd, pushing it past the tip. Paint the area above the hat brim Black. Paint the hat brim Black.

PREPARING GOURDS

Gourds must be thoroughly dry before they can be painted. Because the drying process takes several months, gourds purchased in fall won't be ready for display by Christmas season—so plan well ahead. To dry gourds, place them in a dry, well-ventilated room. Don't drill holes into them until they are completely dry. The holes invite bacteria and may cause them to rot. Also, keep in mind that some gourds you buy will rot no matter how carefully you tend them.

When the gourds are dry, they will be very lightweight; you may hear seeds rattling. The outer skin will be moldy and dried on the surface, so it must be scrubbed to remove it. If possible, leave the gourds in the rain for several hours to loosen their skins. Fill a bucket with warm, soapy water; add a few drops of chlorine bleach to help deter mold spores. Dip and scrub the gourds with a copper scouring pad until they're clean. Place clean gourds in a well-ventilated area for several days to dry out again. To hasten the process, place them in an oven at 200° for about two hours.

Once the gourds are dry, paint them with a mix of equal parts of sealer and Delta Quaker Gray 2057 acrylic paint. The paint seals the surface, allows the next layer of paint to adhere better, and covers any remaining mold stains. It also opaques any red or white paint you plan to use. Let dry; paint the gourd as desired.

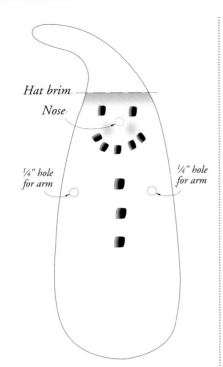

Diagram 2: Gourd Schematic

Hat brim

Nose

¼" hole for arm

¼" hole for arm

Referring to Diagram 2, *above,* paint the eyes, mouth, and buttons Black and highlight them with White. Using AO and the dry scrubber, color the cheeks. Allow the paint to dry.

Drill a small hole through the top of the gourd for a raffia tie hanger. Drill an arm hole in each side of the gourd for the tree twig arms.

Spray the gourd with the matte sealer; apply the antiquing medium and let dry. To finish the snowman, varnish the entire piece, including the hat brim.

Decorate the hat band by tying and gluing a 1"-wide length of torn fabric around the gourd just above the brim. Adhere bits of artificial garland and berries all around the hat brim.

Insert a length of raffia through the holes in the hat, and tie the ends together for a hanging loop.

Insert the tree twigs into the arm holes. Glue the orange-compound nose to the face with the Goop glue.
—*Designed by Jeri Francis of Fiddlestix*

SNOWMEN FRIENDS FLOORCLOTH

Shown on page 52 and right. The finished floorcloth is 28×36".

YOU WILL NEED:

Patterns opposite

28×36" piece of artist's canvas

Gesso and sponge brush

Fine-grit sandpaper

Masking tape

Delta Ceramcoat Acrylic paint: Antique Gold 2002 (AN), Barn Red 2490 (BN), Black 2506, Black Green 2116 (BG), Candy Bar 2407 (CB), Chambray Blue 2514 (HL), Forest Green 2010 (FG), Georgia Clay 2097 (GC), Hippo Gray 2090 (HG), Light Ivory 2401 (LI), and Sweetheart Blush 2130 (SB)

Paintbrushes: Liners #10/0 and #1, small flat #2, large flat #14, round #4, and 1" sponge

Graphite transfer paper

Tracing paper

Stylus

Matte acrylic varnish

Paste wax

INSTRUCTIONS

Prepare the artist's canvas surface with a coat of Gesso using the sponge brush. Let dry; lightly sand the surface. Paint the entire surface HL. Lightly sand the painted surface. Apply a second coat and sand again, if necessary. Measure a 1½"-wide outside border all around the canvas and tape it off. Paint the border BN. Let the paint dry; remove the tape.

Transfer the border design to the BN border; paint with AN and FG dots. Measure 4½" from the inside border, and tape off a second ¼"-wide border. Paint the border FG.

Referring to the photograph, *above right,* for placement, transfer four snowmen to each end, six snowmen to each side, and Snowflake A to each corner between the BN and FG

borders. Base-coat the snowmen's bodies and snowflakes LI. Referring to the photograph, *page 52,* for color placement, alternate the colors for the snowmen's hats, mittens, and scarves as follows. For one set, base-coat the scarf, mittens, and hat brim FG; shade with BG. Line the plaid scarf BN. Line the mitten ribbing Black. Base-coat the hat top FG. For another set, base-coat the scarf, mittens, and hat brim BN. Mix SB and CB 3:1 and shade the scarf, mittens, and hat brim. Line the plaid scarf FG. Line the mitten ribbing Black. Base-coat the hat top FG.

Base-coat the noses GC. Paint the eyes with Black crosshatch. Using the stylus, dot the ends of the crosshatch lines Black.

Transfer three of the Snowflake B and five of the Snowflake C patterns to the floorcloth center. Base-coat the snowflakes with LI. Paint the falling snow in the center and around the snowmen with LI dots. Using HG, add "commas" to outline the snow dots; let dry. Apply several coats of varnish to the surface of the floorcloth with a sponge brush; let dry. For protection and easy cleaning of the floorcloth, apply paste wax to the surface with a soft cloth.
—*Designed by Leslie Beck of Fiber Mosaics*

SNOWMAN FRIENDS
FLOORCLOTH PATTERNS

Snowflake B

Snowflake A

Snowflake C

HEAVENLY SNOWMAN
ANGEL PATTERNS

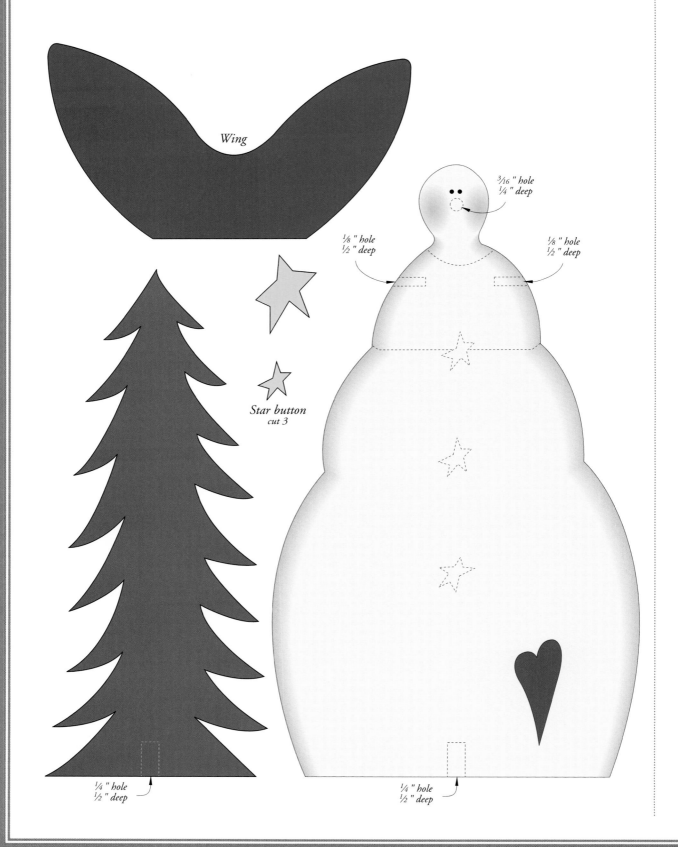

Wing

Star button
cut 3

³⁄₁₆ " hole
¹⁄₄ " deep

¹⁄₈ " hole
¹⁄₂ " deep

¹⁄₈ " hole
¹⁄₂ " deep

¹⁄₄ " hole
¹⁄₂ " deep

¹⁄₄ " hole
¹⁄₂ " deep

HEAVENLY SNOWMAN ANGEL

Shown on page 53 *and* below.

YOU WILL NEED:

Patterns opposite

1×6×8" pine
⅛×3×6" Baltic birch plywood
³⁄₁₆×1" dowel
Scrollsaw and #5R blade
Drill and drill bits
100- and 150-grit sandpaper
Tack cloth, cotton swab, and wood sealer
Paintbrushes: Loew-Cornell ¾" synthetic flat, #6 synthetic flat, #3 synthetic round, and spatter or old toothbrush
Delta Ceramcoat Colors Acrylic paint: Antique White 2001 (AW), Black 2506, Burgundy Rose 2123 (BR), Burnt Umber 2025 (BU), Dark Forest 2096 (DF), Pigskin 2093 (PS), and Terra Cotta 2071 (TC)
Antiquing medium and 5-minute epoxy
Satin-finish varnish
2—#7×1⅛" flathead screws
32" length of 20-gauge black wire
½×18" strip of fabric
1"-diameter miniature black felt hat

INSTRUCTIONS

Transfer the outlines of the snowman and the tree from the patterns onto 1" pine (actual thickness: ¾") and draw a 2×8½" rectangle for the base onto the pine.

Copy the wings, the large star, and three small stars onto ⅛" Baltic birch plywood. Cut out the shapes with a scrollsaw, using a #5R blade.

For the snowman's nose, sand or sharpen one end of the dowel to a point, then trim it to measure ¾". Drill all holes where shown on the pattern. Sand all surfaces with 100- and then 150-grit sandpaper. Remove the sanding dust with a tack cloth.

Apply wood sealer to all surfaces, and let dry. Sand again with 150-grit sandpaper and wipe clean.

Base-coat only the front surfaces of all cutouts except the base, which needs to have all surfaces base-coated except the bottom. Using a ¾" flat brush, base-coat the snowman AW, the tree DF, and the base and wings BR. Use a #6 flat brush to base-coat the stars PS and the nose TC. Let dry, then lightly sand with a paper grocery sack to remove fuzz raised by the paint; remove sanding dust.

Using a ¾" flat brush, float BU shading along all outer edges of the snowman except across the bottom. Dip a cotton swab in BR, and wipe off most of the paint on a paper towel; with a circular motion, use the swab to blush the snowman's cheeks. Use a #3 round brush to paint the heart BR with two comma strokes. Dot the eyes Black. Dilute Black with water to ink consistency. Dip a spatter brush or an old toothbrush into the diluted paint, and spatter (flyspeck) the snowman, wings, base, and tree.

Apply antiquing medium to all surfaces of the cutouts; let dry. Sand spots of paint from the front of the snowman where the stars will join and from the back of the snowman and the front of the wings where those pieces will join. (Glue and epoxy don't bond permanently to painted or varnished surfaces.)

Epoxy the nose, small stars, and wings in place; let set. Apply one or more coats of varnish, allowing drying time between coats.

Attach the snowman and tree to the base with screws. Cut the wire into eight 4" lengths. To make each arm, loosely twist four strands of wire together. Dip one end of each arm in epoxy, and insert in the holes in the snowman's sides. Separate the wires at the other end to form the hand. Epoxy the large star to the snowman's right hand, and bend to shape the arms as shown in the photograph, *page 53.*

Tear a strip of fabric; tie it in a bow around the snowman's neck. Epoxy the felt hat to the snowman's head.

—Designed by Jan Shirley

FAMILY
🌿 TREE 🌿

*F*amily collections including
linens, buttons, teacups, and jewelry are treasured
even more when incorporated into ornaments and
adornments for stockings. Turn broken family
china into the pieces of a beautiful mosaic tray.
Make wonderful ornaments and gift wrap for all to
enjoy using color photocopies of old photographs,
cherished embroideries, and vintage lace.

Instructions begin on page 84.

HEIRLOOM PACKAGE WRAPS

Antique family linens, embroidery, and quilts make any gift
extra special when color-photocopied to make wrapping paper.
Attach old jewelry and other keepsakes for added nostalgia.

SILVER SPOONS

Give an old spoon new life as an ornament for your Christmas
tree. Begin by washing and polishing your collection of vintage
spoons. Larger spoons hook over tree branches by bending the
handle around a dowel, a large magic marker, or a tool designed
to bend pipe. A lovely ribbon bow in your Christmas colors
adds an elegant and coordinated touch.

CRYSTAL CROCHETED ORNAMENTS

Use two matching heirloom doilies to make this exquisite
ornament that's adorned with a chandelier or crystal prism
tassel. Weave silk ribbon to join the edges, stuff
with fiberfill, and add a pretty bow.
Instructions are on page 84.

DAINTY DEMITASSE SPOONS

A tiny dried rose and a bit of greenery glued to
the bowl of a dainty demitasse spoon makes a pretty
little ornament for the tree.

HEIRLOOM LACE ORNAMENTS

Preserve the lace your grandmother lovingly
crafted by turning it into a special ornament.
Use fabric stiffener to make the ornament
more durable; and add a beaded tassel
and a ribbon bow for the finishing touches.

RIBBON-AND-BUTTON TASSEL

Reach into your collection of old buttons and showcase
a favorite one by transforming it into a pretty ribbon
tassel, *opposite*, using sheer and satin ribbons.
Instructions are on page 87.

MINI PICTURE FRAMES

Turn any small frame into a display
for your old photos. Don't rule out frames
that aren't the right color—you can paint
them. For wooden frames, attach a small screw
eye to the center top of the frame, and add
ribbons and an ornament hanger. If desired,
add a second screw eye at the center bottom of
the frame to attach a beaded tassel. Embellish
the front of the frame with charms, old
jewelry, buttons, and other decorations.

PHOTOCOPY ORNAMENTS

Capture memories of loved ones with these easy-to-make
ornaments. Make color photocopies of old photographs, crop
them to the desired size, and add lace trim and a ribbon hanger.
Or combine a photocopy of an antique linen or quilt
with a copy of the relative who made it.

TREASURED TEACUPS

Bring out your family china collection and display the teacups
on the boughs of your tree. Slip a length of silk ribbon through the
teacup handle and tie it to the branches with a bow.

MONOGRAMMED HANKIE ORNAMENT

Folded diagonally in half and cinched near the top with an elegant ribbon bow, monogrammed handkerchiefs, *opposite*, make pretty ornaments for the tree at Christmas time.

PRESSED-TIN ORNAMENTS

Some of the earliest photographs were delivered from photographers in ornate pressed-tin frames. You can craft these decorative framed photos, *opposite*, into ornaments by adhering a simple silk ribbon bow to the top of the frame and hanging it with an ornament hanger.

WRAPPED HANDKERCHIEF ORNAMENT

Display heirloom handkerchiefs by crafting them into creative ornaments. Using a 6"-diameter plastic-foam ball, glue a loop of ribbon onto the ball for a hanger, wrap a pretty lace-edged handkerchief around the ball, and cinch it closed with ribbon. The ends of the handkerchief create an attractive ruffle at the top of the ornament.

HANDKERCHIEF TASSEL ORNAMENT

Make a tassel using a pretty handkerchief and a miniature flower pot for the base. Instructions are on page 87.

JEWELED STOCKINGS

Reach into the family scrap bag and make these
creative stockings using old doilies and decorative fabrics.
Vintage jewelry doubles as buttons and fringe, and add a sparkling
touch to your holiday finery. Instructions are on page 85.

VINTAGE PLATES MOSAIC TRAY

Turn bits of broken family china into an elegant mosaic design
on the top of a serving tray. Instructions are on page 86.

VINTAGE JEWELRY ORNAMENTS

Sparkling rhinestones that adorn old costume jewelry
twinkle in the glow of the lights upon your tree.
These stunning ornaments are easier to make than you
may think—hook an antique chandelier prism or
crystal onto the bottom of a brooch or earring, and
insert an ornament hook in the top of the
jewelry for a quick decoration.

CRYSTAL CROCHETED ORNAMENT

Shown on page 76 *and* right.
The finished ornament is 4¾×6".

CROCHET ABBREVIATIONS

beg—begin(ning)
bet—between
bl—block
ch(s)—chain(s)
dc—double crochet
lp(s)—loop(s)
rep—repeat
rnd(s)—round(s)
sc—single crochet
sk—skip
sl st—slip stitch
sp—space
*—repeat whatever follows the * as indicated
( )—work directions given in parentheses
 the number of times indicated

YOU WILL NEED:

50-g ball of cotton crochet thread in ecru
Size 10 (1.15mm) steel crochet hook or size
 needed to obtain gauge
3" square of lightweight fleece
Chenille and beading needles
1 yard of 1½"-wide silk ribbon
⅓ yard of ¾"-wide ivory satin ribbon
Ecru sewing thread
½ yard of ⅛"-wide moss green ribbon
Four coordinating decorative beads
Heirloom crystal or chandelier prism

INSTRUCTIONS

Note: *Use two heirloom crocheted doilies or crochet two matching doilies for each ornament desired.*

Crochet the Doilies

Beg at center, ch 6; join with sl st to form ring.

Rnd 1: Ch 3 (counts as dc), dc in ring; (ch 2, 2 dc in ring) 7 times, ch 2; join with sl st in third ch of beg ch-3; turn.

Rnd 2: [Ch 3 (counts as dc), in first ch-2 sp (dc, ch 3, 2 dc) = beg corner made]; * (ch 2, sk 2 dc = sp over bl made), in next ch-2 sp (3 dc = bl over sp made), sp over bl **, in next ch-2 sp (2 dc, ch 3, 2 dc = corner made); rep from * around, ending last rep at **; join and turn.

Rnd 3: [Ch 3 (counts as dc), 2 dc in first ch-2 sp = beg bl over sp made], * sp over bl, bl over sp, sp over bl, corner **, sp over bl, bl over sp; rep from * around, ending last rep at **, sp over bl; join and turn.

Rnd 4: Beg bl over sp, sp over bl; * corner, sp over bl **, (bl over sp, sp over bl) 3 times; rep from * around, ending last rep at **, (bl over sp, sp over bl) twice; join and turn.

Rnd 5: Beg bl over sp; * (sp over bl, bl over sp) twice, sp over bl, corner **, (sp over bl, bl over sp) twice; rep from * around, ending last rep at **, sp over bl, bl over sp, sp over bl; join and turn.

Rnd 6: Beg bl over sp; * sp over bl, bl over sp, sp over bl, corner **, (sp over bl, bl over sp) 4 times; rep from * around, ending last rep at **, (sp over bl, bl over sp) 3 times, sp over bl; join and turn.

Rnd 7: Beg bl over sp; * (sp over bl, bl over sp) 3 times, sp over bl, corner **, (sp over bl, bl over sp) 3 times, rep from * around, ending last rep at **, (sp over bl, bl over sp) twice, sp over bl; join and turn.

Rnd 8: Beg bl over sp; * (sp over bl, bl over sp) twice, sp over bl, corner **, (sp over bl, bl over sp) 5 times; rep from * around, ending last rep at **, (sp over bl, bl over sp) 4 times, sp over bl; join and turn.

Rnd 9: Beg bl over sp; * (sp over bl, bl over sp) 4 times, sp over bl, corner **, (sp over bl, bl over sp) 4 times, rep from * around, ending last rep at **, (sp over bl, bl over sp) 3 times, sp over bl; join and turn.

Rnd 10: Beg bl over sp; * (sp over bl, bl over sp) 3 times, sp over bl, corner **, (sp over bl, bl over sp) 6 times; rep from * around, ending last rep at **, (sp over bl, bl over sp) 5 times, sp over bl; join and turn.

Rnd 11: In first ch of ch-2 sp [sl st, ch 3 (counts as dc)], dc in next ch; * dc in each of next 3 dc **, dc in each of next 2 ch; rep from * across to corner (dc in next 2 dc, dc in each of 3 ch, dc in next 2 dc), dc in each of next 2 ch; rep from * around, ending last rep at **; join.

Rnd 12: Ch 5 (counts as dc, ch 2); * sk 2 dc, dc in next dc, ch 2; rep from * around; join with sl st in third ch of beg ch-5.

Rnd 13: Ch 1, sc in same st as join; * 2 sc in ch-2 sp, sc in dc; rep from * around, ending 2 sc in last ch-2 sp; join with sl st in first sc.

For picot edging: ***With right side facing, join yarn with sl st in any sc. (Ch 3, sk 2 sc, sl st in next sc) twice; turn; in first ch-3 sp (4 sc, ch 3, sl st in 4th sc for picot, 3 sc in same ch-3 sp), 7 sc in next ch-3 sp, sl st in same sc as joining sl st; turn; ch 1, sl st in each of first 4 sc, ch 3, sl st in last sl st for picot, sl st in next sc, ch 6, sk 4 sc, sl st in next sc; turn; in ch-6 lp (5 sc, picot, sc, picot, sc, picot, 5 sc), sl st in base of picot. Fasten off ***. (Sk 5 sc to left of last decoration, work bet ***) around—18 total decorations.

Finish the Ornament

Lay the two crocheted doilies together with wrong sides out and a 3"-square of lightweight fleece sandwiched between the layers. Using a chenille needle and referring to the photograph *opposite,* sew the two doilies together by weaving a 15"-long piece of silk ribbon through the outer border of the ornament. Thread a 15"-long piece of ribbon through the top corner of the ornament and tie it into a bow.

Cut the ivory ribbon into three 3"-long pieces. Fold each piece into a V-shape as shown in the photograph. Sew the three folded ivory pieces just below the ribbon bow. Tie the moss green ribbon into a bow and sew it on the center top of the folded ivory ribbon pieces. Sew a small bead on top of the green ribbon.

To make the beaded tassel, thread a beading needle with ecru sewing thread and attach it to the bottom corner of the ornament. Thread four decorative beads onto the needle, stitch through the crystal or prism, and then bring the threaded needle back up through all of the beads and finish by attaching it to the bottom corner of the ornament.

JEWELED STOCKINGS
Shown on page 82 *and* left.
The stockings are 18" long.

YOU WILL NEED:
Pattern on page 38

Tracing paper
½ yard of tapestry or jacquard fabric
Old doilies or ¼ yard of contrasting fabric
½ yard of lining fabric
12" length of coordinating silk ribbon
Old costume jewelry such as brooches or necklaces
Coordinated sewing thread and sewing needle

INSTRUCTIONS

Trace the stocking pattern onto tracing paper. Add a ½" seam allowance all around the stocking. Cut out the completed pattern piece.

Cut a matching stocking front and back from the tapestry or jacquard fabric. With the right sides facing and using a ½" seam allowance, sew the stocking front to the back, leaving the top edge open. **Note:** *If desired, add an old doily to the toe or heel for decoration.* Clip the curves and turn the stocking right side out. Finger-press the seam.

Note: *For the cuff, use either an old doily or sew a more traditional cuff using the directions that follow.*

Cut a 6×17" rectangle from the cuff fabric and a matching lining from the lining fabric. Fold the cuff in half crosswise with right sides facing; sew together along the short sides.

Press the seam open, and turn right side out. Sew and press the lining in the same way.

Slip the lining over the cuff with the right sides facing. Sew together along the bottom edge. Trim the seam allowance, and turn right side out.

Slip the lined cuff or doily over the top of the stocking (with the cuff lining facing the right side of the stocking), matching raw edges. Stitch the cuff or doily to the stocking.

For the lining, cut out a stocking front and back from the lining fabric. With the right sides facing, sew the lining pieces together, leaving the top edge and one side open for turning. Do not turn right side out.

Slip the stocking into the lining with the right sides facing; sew completely around the opening.

Turn the stocking right side out through the lining opening. Slip-stitch the opening closed, then slip the lining inside the stocking.

Open out the cuff. Keeping the cuff free, topstitch through the stocking and lining ¼" from the seam line around the top edge. Turn cuff down.

Fold the silk ribbon in half for the hanging loop; sew the ends to the top left edge of the cuff.

Trim the cuff with old costume jewelry. Pin brooches directly onto the cuff, or hand-stitch necklaces around the bottom edge.

VINTAGE PLATES MOSAIC TRAY

Shown on page 83 and above.
The tray is 12×20".

YOU WILL NEED:

Wooden tray (new unfinished or antique)
Medium- and fine-grit sandpaper
Tack cloth
Broken china or tile
Tile adhesive or 5-minute epoxy
Plaid Mosaic Grout (this 12×20" tray took 2 pounds of grout)
Mosaic Colorant (optional)
Spatula or spreading tool
Sponge
Acrylic paint in colors to accent your china or tile
Flat paintbrushes
Four finials or wooden balls for feet
Varnish
Braid to go around your tray plus 2"
Brass upholstery tacks

INSTRUCTIONS

Prepare the Tray

Note: For ease in working and to avoid damaging the decorative surface of the tray, don't paint the tray or attach the feet until the mosaic is completed.

Sand the surface of a new unfinished or antique tray. If the tray you select has been varnished or painted, sand the surface to create "tack." Remember that glue and epoxy won't bond permanently to surfaces that are coated with paint or varnish. Use medium- and then fine-grit sandpaper to remove the paint or varnish from the areas where you plan to attach the feet.

Remove all of the sanding dust with a tack cloth.

Apply the Mosaic

Use broken vintage plates, or break your own china following the instructions *opposite*. Using the tile adhesive or 5-minute epoxy, apply the broken pieces in a pleasing manner. For the tray shown, our designer used a pencil to draw the borders and the inside circles. Space the broken china pieces consistently. Let the adhesive dry thoroughly.

Mix the grout according to the manufacturer's instructions.

While the grout is wet, tint it to the color of your choice if desired. For the light teal grout on our design, we used drops of Blue Sapphire and Emerald Green Mosaic Colorant, adding only a small amount of color at a time. You'll need to work fast— the grout sets up quickly.

Using a spatula or any spreading tool, work the grout in between the broken china pieces. Allow the grout to set for approximately 10 to 15 minutes. Using a sponge, wipe off the excess grout to expose the mosaic design. Rinse the sponge often.

Note: Don't get discouraged as you wipe the grout off the design. The cleaning process is slow as the wet grout is smeared over the china or tile pieces. Once the grout is smooth and the china is relatively clean, let the grout dry to harden. Polish away any grout dust from the china or tile using a soft cloth.

Finish the Tray

With acrylic paint, base-coat the tray sides and rim using colors that coordinate with your mosaic design.

Paint the feet a solid color, then decorate with a freehand-painted design of vine and leaves if desired.

Finish the painted surfaces with two coats of acrylic varnish, allowing the surfaces to dry between coats.

Attach the braid trim to the edge of the tray with upholstery tacks so it can easily be removed for cleaning.

Overlap the braid along one end and add an upholstery tack to finish.

Note: *Apply a bead of glue to both ends before you cut your braid. When the glue dries, cut through the glue area, and the braid won't unravel.*

HANDKERCHIEF TASSEL
Shown on page 81 *and* right.

YOU WILL NEED:
Acrylic paint in coordinating color
Disposable foam paintbrush
¾"-diameter wooden bead
7" length of coordinating ¼"-wide satin ribbon
Vintage handkerchief
Sewing needle
Coordinating sewing thread
Size 5 metal crochet hook or size to fit through hole of wooden bead
1 yard of coordinating cord
1½"-tall, 1¼"-diameter wooden flower pot
Glue gun and hotmelt adhesive
13—½"-wide ribbon roses in matching color

INSTRUCTIONS
Paint the ¾"-diameter wooden bead with coordinating acrylic paint. Let the bead dry.

Fold the satin ribbon in half and tie the ends together in an overhand knot. Set the loop aside.

Fold the handkerchief in half, then fold it in half again with the center pointing up. Hand-stitch the satin-ribbon knot onto the center point of the handkerchief. Using a crochet hook, pull the loop of the satin ribbon up through the center of the flower pot and the bead. Tie an overhand knot in the satin ribbon at the top of the wooden bead to prevent the loop from slipping back through the bead and flower pot.

Wind the cord around the bottom edge of the flower pot, adhering it with a thin line of hotmelt adhesive.

Embellish the tassel by adhering a few ribbon roses to the center of the cord-wrapped flower pot. Apply more roses around the base of the bead and to the base of the ribbon loop.

RIBBON-AND-BUTTON TASSEL
Shown on page 79.

YOU WILL NEED:
½ yard of coordinating ¼"-wide satin ribbon
2—18" lengths of sheer ribbons in coordinating colors
Glue gun and hotmelt adhesive
1¾"-diameter decorative button
½"-wide ribbon rose in coordinating color

INSTRUCTIONS
Fold a 6" length of satin ribbon in half, and tie the ends together in an overhand knot.

Hold the two sheer ribbons together, and fold them in half. Pinch the sheer ribbons together approximately 2" from the fold, and glue the knot of the satin ribbon onto the back of the folded sheer ribbon.

Hold the button on top of the ribbon, on the opposite side of the knot. Attach the button by threading the remaining length of satin ribbon through the holes of the button, going from the front to the back, over the knot, and through to the front side of the button. Tie the ribbon into a bow on the front side of the button. Glue a small ribbon rose to the middle of the bow.

BREAKING CHINA
Here's a great way to make a clean break. You'll need a wooden cutting board, a paper grocery bag, a hammer, and your plates or tiles. Choose pieces of china or tile that have flat surfaces, since you'll lose any areas that have a ridge or curve. For a mosaic tray or table top, select plates or tiles that are of equal thickness so that the surface is flat.

Lay the bag on its side on the cutting board (working on a carpeted floor muffles the sound), and open the bag enough to slide your plate, saucer, or tile inside. Close the bag over the plate, and tap the china with the hammer until you get pieces of a desirable size. The pieces in the tray range from ½" to 1" wide.

Open the bag, remove the pieces that are right for your mosaic, and continue to break those that are too large. Once you've picked out all the pieces that will work for your project, simply set the bag on end and let the remnants fall to the bottom. Continue in this manner. When you're finished, throw the bag and the waste away.

WHITE
🌿CHRISTMAS🌿

*G*littery paper snowflakes

arranged in a vase, *opposite*, set the scene for a white

Christmas decorating theme. Accents such as a

pears-and-roses wreath, velvet and vintage-linen

stockings, and a snowflake table runner add

elegance. Also craft a patchwork pillow, cross-stitch

snowflake ornaments, and sew a rag doll angel

worked in visions of white.

Instructions begin on page 100.

VINTAGE-LINEN MINI STOCKING

Good things come in small stockings! This mini stocking,
trimmed with vintage linen and buttons, works up fast. Make a
few at a time, and fill them with favors for your holiday guests.
Instructions are on page 110.

MOSAIC BUTTON BALL ORNAMENT

Cute as a button, this lovely ornament unites silver silk leaves, sheer ribbon,
and, of course, an assortment of white buttons——all adhered to a plastic-
foam ball. Instructions are on page 113.

TWINKLING BOWL DECORATION

Silver balls and beaded garland with crystal stars in a glass bowl
are ready to be plucked for trimming the tree or
admired for their beauty.

PEARS-AND-ROSES WREATH

Adorn a ring of greens with fruit and florals, *opposite*, to celebrate
the bounty of the season. Our arrangement of pears and roses
forms a cheery wreath to display anywhere in
your holiday home. Instructions are on page 112.

JINGLE BELL CANDLE SHADE

This holiday decoration has a familiar ring: Jingle bells dangle from
a shade atop a white candlestick lamp perfectly suited for a white Christmas
theme grouping. Instructions are on page 112.

FROSTED ICE-CREAM CONE ORNAMENT

Here's a decorating treat. Top an ice-cream cone with
modeling compound, and paint it with white acrylic paint to create
a delectable ornament. Don't forget to add the bead "sprinkles"!
Instructions are on page 103.

PATCHWORK TREE PILLOW

Delight holiday guests
with your hand-
stitched patchwork
pillow. Embellished
with gold metallic
trims suggesting
garlands and ornament
balls, the glittery
Christmas tree motif
coordinates with the
cream-colored fabric
border—just the right
combination of accents
to suit your taste
and a white
Christmas theme.
Instructions are
on page 109.

VELVET-TRIMMED BUTTON STOCKING

An elegant addition to your holiday mantel, this velvet-trimmed stocking
is fashioned with jacquard fabric and vintage buttons. It makes a pretty accessory for your
hearth—especially when you fill it with gold metallic gift-wrapped presents.
Instructions are on page 103.

SHEER SNOWFLAKE TABLE DOILY

It's easy to create this stylish table runner. Simply place a snowflake template
on the material and apply a fabric etching gel to the exposed areas to create an
embossed pattern. Display the piece with white bowls, candlesticks, or vases to
carry out your white Christmas theme. Instructions are on page 100.

WHIMSICAL RAG DOLL ANGEL

Make this charming angel doll dressed in white, silver, and gold to watch over your holiday home. Use our full-size patterns to create the doll, and then embellish her as you please, filling her arms with precious little gifts. Instructions are on page 104.

SNOWFLAKE STITCHERY ORNAMENTS

Cross-stitch three unique snowflake designs on wintry blue Aida cloth, trim them with lovely lace accents, and mount them in clear candle rings for distinctive ornaments. Display them as a set on your Christmas tree, or give some to your family and friends as holiday party favors and fine gifts. Instructions are on page 109.

GLITTERY PAPER SNOWFLAKE DECORATIONS

Shown on page 88 *and* below.
The snowflakes measure 3", 4", 5", and 6" in diameter.

YOU WILL NEED:

Patterns opposite *and on* page 102

Medium-weight fusible transfer paper
1 yard of 45"-wide patterned lace fabric
White poster board
X-ACTO knife
Spray adhesive
Nontarnish iridescent glitter
For each ornament:
15" length of ¹⁄₁₆"-wide opalescent ribbon floss
For the centerpiece:
Wood skewers, painted white
6"-diameter plastic-foam ball
Large urn
Fresh evergreen branches
Several yards of 3"-wide wire-edged
 silver-flocked ribbon

INSTRUCTIONS

Trace the snowflake patterns onto the fusible transfer paper. Fuse the transfer paper to the wrong side of

the lace, following the manufacturer's directions. Using a press cloth, fuse the lace snowflakes onto the poster board. Cut out the snowflakes, using the X-ACTO knife. Spray the lace side of the snowflakes with the adhesive, and sprinkle with the nontarnish iridescent glitter.

For the centerpiece arrangement, carefully push a wood skewer between the lace and poster board of each snowflake. Trim the plastic-foam ball so one side is flat. With the flat side down, place the foam ball in the bottom of the urn. Arrange the evergreen branches and snowflakes by inserting their ends into the foam ball. Tie the silver-flocked ribbon in a bow around the urn.

To make ornaments from the snowflakes, cut a 15" length of the opalescent ribbon floss, fold it in half, and glue the ends together on the back of each snowflake ornament.

—Designed by Margaret Sindelar

SHEER SNOWFLAKE TABLE DOILY

Shown on page 96 *and* above.
The table doily measures 18" square.

YOU WILL NEED:

Patterns opposite *and on* page 102

⅝ yard of batiste-weight 50/50
 cotton/polyester fabric
Silk or 100% polyester sewing thread
Wax-coated freezer paper
Self-adhesive 1"-diameter dots
Straight pins
Rubber gloves
Fiber-Etch fabric remover
Disposable sponge brush
2½ yards of ⅜"-wide white flat braid
4—⅝"-diameter white shank buttons

INSTRUCTIONS

Cut a 22" square from the fabric. Press fabric under 1" twice on all sides and machine-hem.

Trace the snowflake patterns onto the freezer paper. Cut out and arrange

GLITTERY PAPER SNOWFLAKE
DECORATIONS AND SHEER
SNOWFLAKE TABLE DOILY PATTERNS

GLITTERY PAPER SNOWFLAKE
DECORATIONS AND SHEER
SNOWFLAKE TABLE DOILY PATTERNS

the shapes on the hemmed fabric, as desired. Use a warm iron to adhere the snowflakes to the fabric. Add the self-adhesive dots at random.

Working on a surface protected with layers of newspaper, smooth and pin the fabric at the outer edges and through several layers of newspaper.

While wearing rubber gloves, use the Fiber-Etch fabric remover to remove the cotton fibers, following the manufacturer's directions.

Note: *Test a sample of the fabric before working on the project. Squeeze the gel onto a glass plate, then use the sponge brush to carefully apply the gel to the fabric. Apply an ample amount of the gel, and don't distort the snowflakes.*

Remove the pins and the self-adhesive dots, and hang the fabric on a clothesline to dry. Use a blow dryer to speed up the drying process.

Place the dry fabric, covered with a press cloth, on a protected ironing surface. Iron the fabric until it is light brown. Rinse the fabric and remove the paper snowflakes.

Let the fabric dry, then iron with a press cloth and a cool iron.

Topstitch a length of braid along the top and bottom hems. Repeat for the sides. Sew the buttons to the corners where the braids cross.

Note: *Use a warm iron and a press cloth when ironing the table doily.*
—*Designed by Margaret Sindelar*

FROSTED ICE-CREAM CONE ORNAMENT

Shown on page 94 *and left.*
The finished ornament is 5" tall.

YOU WILL NEED:
Spray acrylic sealer
Sugar cone
Glue gun and hotmelt adhesive
2"-diameter plastic-foam ball
Liquitex Acrylic Modeling Paste
Sponge brush
White and light-tan acrylic crafts paint
Gold seed beads
8" length of narrow metallic-gold cord
2 metallic-gold daisy sequins

INSTRUCTIONS
Spray the sugar cone with the sealer so it won't become soggy when you paint. Glue the foam ball into the cone; "frost" the ball with the modeling paste. Let it dry. Using a sponge brush, paint the ball white; immediately sprinkle it with beads. Let it dry. Paint the cone light tan; let it dry. Spray the painted cone with sealer. For the hanger, glue the ends of the cord to the sides of the cone; glue a daisy sequin over each end.
—*Designed by Jim Williams*

VELVET-TRIMMED BUTTON STOCKING

Shown on page 97 *and* 104.
The finished stocking is 19½" long.

YOU WILL NEED:
Pattern on page 105

Tracing paper
½ yard of white woven-print satin fabric
½ yard of white basketweave-textured fabric
⅜ yard of off-white velvet
½ yard of cream stripe fabric
2 yards of ¼"-diameter cording
Matching sewing threads
3—1"-diameter gold-and-white buttons

INSTRUCTIONS

Note: Use ½" seam allowances for all stitching, unless otherwise noted.

Trace the stocking body and lining pattern onto tracing paper, and add a ½" seam allowance all around. Cut out the completed pattern piece.

Cut out a stocking front and a stocking back from the white woven-print satin fabric. Cut two lining pieces and a 3¾×6" strip for the hanger from the white basketweave-textured fabric. Cut a 13×16" rectangle from the velvet for the cuff.

Cut and piece the cream stripe fabric into a 2"-wide bias strip about 50" long. Press the seams on the strip open. Cover the cording with the bias strip, and stitch it in place to complete the piping.

Matching the raw edges, pin and stitch the piping around the stocking front (except for the top edge). Clip the curves so the piping lies flat.

With the right sides facing, pin and stitch the stocking front and back together. Trim the seam allowance, and clip the curves. Turn the stocking right side out, and press carefully.

With the right sides facing, pin and stitch the lining pieces together, leaving the top edge open. Trim the seam allowance to about ⅛", and clip the curves. Don't turn the lining right side out. Press the lining.

Insert the lining into the stocking. Turn under the raw edge on the opening of the lining. Do the same on the stocking. Pin the lining to the stocking around the opening. Topstitch ⅛" from the edge around the opening. Set the stocking aside.

Press under the seam allowance on the short raw edges of the velvet cuff rectangle. Fold the cuff in half lengthwise with the wrong sides facing. Insert a 15" length of cording centered in the fold of the cuff. Topstitch close to the cording to hold it in place. Turn the cuff so the right sides are facing, and stitch the long raw edges together. Turn the cuff right side out.

Fold the cuff in half, bringing the short edges together. Pin the edges together so they just meet. Slip the cuff over the top of the stocking with the pinned seam in the back. Adjust the cuff as necessary, and pin it in place. Set the stocking aside. Fold the hanger strip in half lengthwise, and

press it. Open up the strip, and press the long raw edges to the center. Fold the strip in half lengthwise again, concealing the raw edges, and topstitch about ⅛" from the long edges. Fold the hanger strip in half crosswise; pin the raw edges between the cuff and the stocking.

Slip-stitch the cuff to the stocking, catching the hanger in the stitching. Slip-stitch the back seam.

Hand-sew the three buttons to the right side of the stocking front.

—*Designed by Jim Williams*

WHIMSICAL RAG DOLL ANGEL

Shown on pages 99 and 107. The finished doll is 21" tall.

YOU WILL NEED:
Patterns on page 106

Body:
Tracing paper
½ yard of unbleached muslin
Polyester fiberfill
12" length of 2"-wide metallic gold ribbon
2 black coquille beads
Rose embroidery floss
Embroidery, beading, and tapestry needles
Powder blush and brush applicator
1 yard of narrow metallic gold cord
Metallic gold thread
8 pearl beads

Dress and detail:
½ yard of white woven-print satin
Elastic thread
½ yard of white tulle
¾ yard of 1"-wide white satin ribbon
Silver foil florist's leaves
2 yards of narrow metallic gold braid
Glue gun and hotmelt adhesive
1 yard of 4"-wide gold-flecked white mesh ribbon
Medium-weight white paper
Fiskars' decorative scalloped-edged scissors
Gold tinsel garland
Metallic silver chenille stem

INSTRUCTIONS

Trace the body, arm, and leg pattern pieces onto tracing paper, and add a ½" seam allowance all around. Cut out the completed pattern pieces.

Cut the body, arm, and leg pieces from the unbleached muslin.

Stitch the Doll Body
Note: Stitch the pieces together with right sides facing and using ½" seam allowances, unless otherwise noted.

VELVET-TRIMMED BUTTON
STOCKING PATTERN

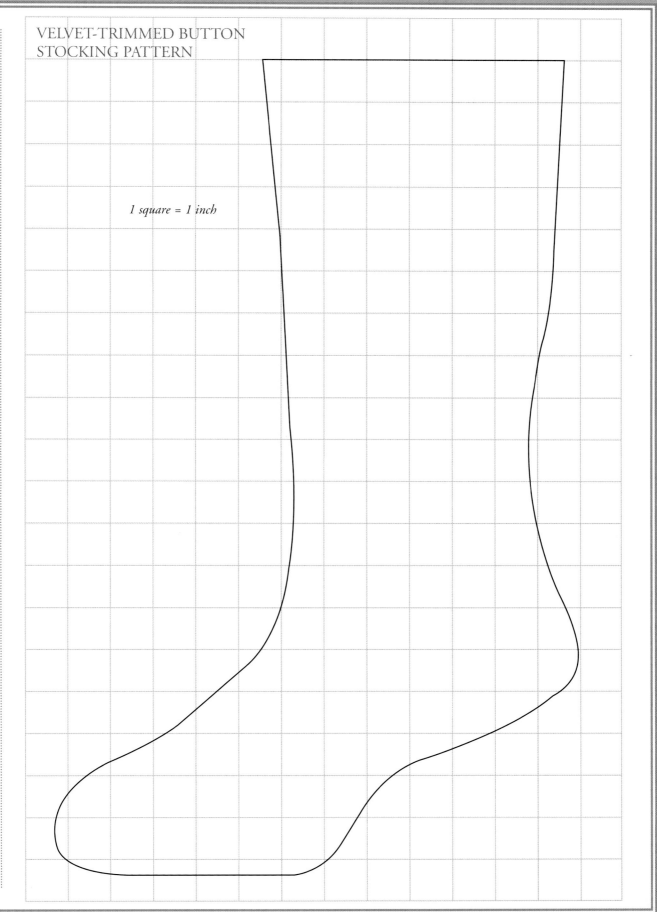

1 square = 1 inch

WHIMSICAL RAG DOLL ANGEL PATTERNS

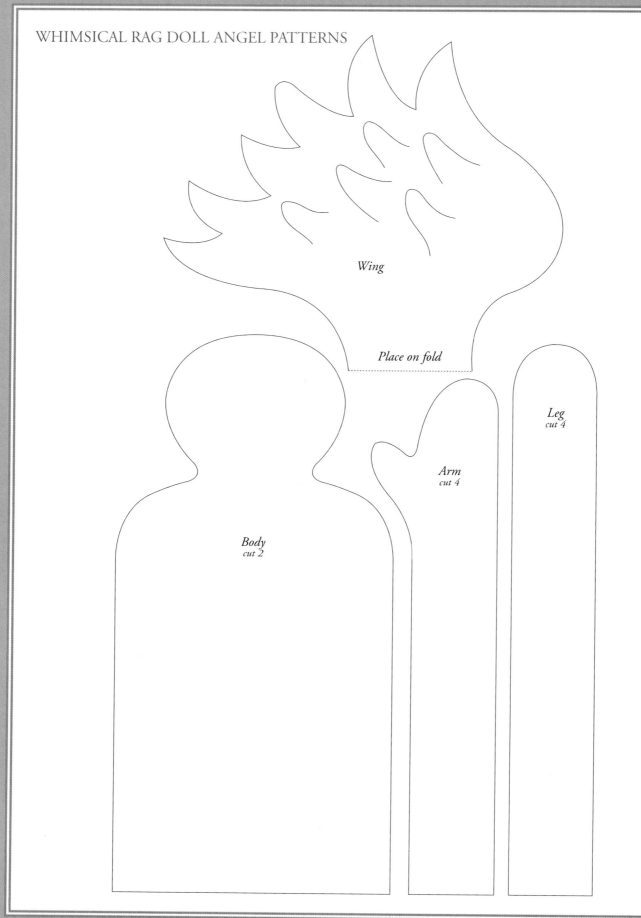

Wing

Place on fold

Leg
cut 4

Arm
cut 4

Body
cut 2

Pin and stitch the body pieces together, leaving openings for the arms, as indicated on the pattern piece, and an opening at the bottom edge for the legs. Trim the seam allowance to ⅛". Clip the curves and turn the body right side out. Press the shape, turning under raw edges ½".

Pin and stitch the arms together in pairs, leaving them open at the straight shoulder edges. Trim the seam allowances to ⅛". Clip the curves, turn the arms right side out, and press. Topstitch the fingers, then lightly stuff the fingers, hands, and arms up to the elbows with the polyester fiberfill.

Topstitch across the arms to create the elbow joints. Stuff the remainder of the arms, and set them aside.

Cut the metallic gold ribbon into four 3" pieces for the slippers. Pin and baste one piece of ribbon to each leg over the toes, placing the finished edges of the ribbons at the top and bottom. Trim excess ribbon.

Pin and stitch the legs together in pairs, leaving openings at the top straight edges. Trim the seam allowances to ⅛". Clip the curves, turn the legs right side out, and press. Lightly stuff the legs; set them aside.

Stuff the body lightly. Insert the arms into the armholes and topstitch the openings closed, catching the arms in the seams.

Insert the legs into the bottom opening of the body, placing the legs close to the side seams of the body. Topstitch the opening closed, catching the legs in the seam.

For the nose, pinch the fabric together in the center of the face. With the embroidery needle threaded with white thread, take a small stitch through the pinched fabric to create the bridge of the nose. About ½"

down from the bridge of the nose, embroider four or five straight stitches, one on top of the other, to define the nostril area.

Sew the black bead eyes on each side of the bridge of the nose using the threaded beading needle. Embroider two rose bullion stitches to create the lips. Brush the cheeks lightly with the powder blush.

For the slipper laces, cut the narrow gold cord in half. Using the tapestry needle, thread the cord halfway through the leg seam allowances at the top of the ribbon slippers. Lace

the cords up the legs and tie into bows in the front.

Tack the bows through the center knots and into the fabric to keep them from slipping down the legs.

Using the metallic thread, stitch around and through the ring finger three to four times to create a band. Stitch a pearl at the front.

Dress the Doll

Cut the following from white satin fabric: two 3×5" rectangles (for the front bodice); one 6½×5" rectangle (for the back bodice); two 8×8½"

SNOWFLAKE STITCHERY
ORNAMENTS CHARTS

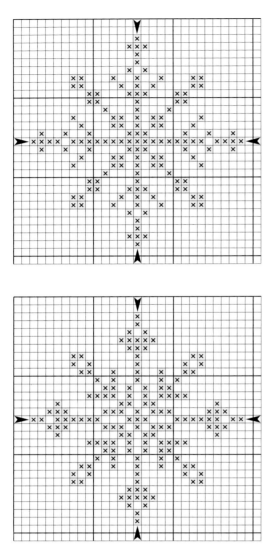

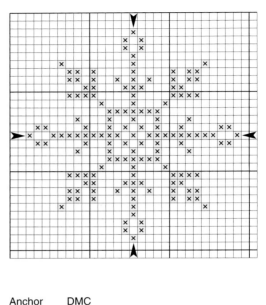

Anchor		DMC	
002	☒	000	White

Stitch count: *27 high x 27 wide*
Finished design sizes:
28-count fabric – 2 x 2 inches
32-count fabric – 1⅝ x 1⅝ inches
36-count fabric – 1½ x 1½ inches

rectangles (for the sleeves), and one 16½"×11" rectangle (for the skirt).

Press under ⅜" on one long side of each front bodice piece, and topstitch close to the folded edge (the hemmed edges are the front opening). With the right sides facing and using ½" for seam allowances, stitch the front bodice pieces to the back bodice at the shoulders, starting at the outer edge and stitching in for 1". Press the seam allowances open.

Press under 1" on one short end of each sleeve rectangle (ruffled cuffs).

Stitch two rows of stitching about ⅛" apart on the cuffs (this is the casing for the ruffled cuffs). With the right sides facing, center the short raw edge of each sleeve to a shoulder seam line on the bodice. Pin and stitch the sleeves to the armhole openings. With the tapestry needle, thread elastic through the cuff casings. Check the fit around the doll's wrists, and knot the elastic to secure it. Sew the sleeve/underarm seams. Sew pearl beads for buttons on the right side of the front bodice.

Place the completed bodice on the doll. Lap the buttoned side over the left front of the bodice, and hand-stitch in place at the lower front.

Press under ½" twice on one long edge of the skirt rectangle; machine-hem. With the right sides together, stitch the short raw edges together. Turn the skirt right side out.

Fold and cut the tulle into six layers that measure about 16½"×11". Pin one long edge of the tulle overskirt to the top edge of the satin skirt. Hand-gather at the waistline. Place the skirt

on the doll. Wrap the satin ribbon around the waist, concealing the raw edges; tie the ribbon at the back.

Wire the silver florist's leaves together to make a 7"-diameter wreath. Wrap gold braid around the wreath ring as a trim. Slip the wreath onto the doll's left arm and stitch the hands into a holding position.

Wrap the mesh ribbon around the doll's shoulders for a stole.

Create the Wings

Trace the wing pattern onto tracing paper and cut out. Trace around the pattern onto the white paper. Transfer the interior feathers by pressing the lines into the paper with an empty pen or a stylus. Cut out the wings using scissors for all of the top cuts. Use the scalloped scissors to cut the underside of the feathers.

Cut the interior feather lines with the X-ACTO blade. Turn the wings over to the wrong side, and pin-prick holes around the interior feathers with a tapestry needle. Roll the edges of the feathers to curl them and give the wings dimension. Glue the wings to the back of the body.

Stitch tinsel garland over the head for the hair. For the halo, coil the silver stem into a 2"-diameter circle, twisting the ends to secure. Stitch the halo at the back of the head.

—*Designed by Jim Williams*

SNOWFLAKE STITCHERY ORNAMENTS

Shown on page 98 *and* left.
The ornaments are 3⅜" in diameter.

YOU WILL NEED:

Charts opposite

For each ornament:
6" square of 28-count Silver Blue Jobelan fabric
DMC white cotton floss
Small embroidery hoop
Embroidery needle
2"-diameter self-covering button
Fusible webbing paper
4" square of fleece
Glue gun and hotmelt adhesive
7" of ½"-wide white lace
3⅜"-diameter clear plastic candle ring
1"-diameter button with two holes
12" of twisted cording

INSTRUCTIONS

Zigzag-stitch or overcast the edges of the fabric to prevent fraying. Find the center of the chart and the center of the fabric; begin stitching there. Use two plies of floss to work the cross-stitches over two threads of the fabric. Place the finished stitchery facedown on a soft towel and press.

Trace the backing circle from the self-covered button package onto the fusible webbing paper. Fuse the webbing paper to the fleece. Cut out the circle, then center and fuse it to the wrong side of the completed stitchery. Cut out the stitchery.

Cover the self-covering button with the stitchery following the manufacturer's instructions. Glue lace trim around the back of the button. Place the covered button in the candle ring with the two-hole button on the back side. Stitch the buttons together with floss. Knot the threads; glue the knot to the two-hole button.

Fold the twisted cording in half, then tie an overhand knot 1" from the fold. Tie a knot at the end of each tail. Slip the knots between the buttons, then glue about 1" of the tails to the back of the candle ring so the ornament will hang straight.

—*Designed by Margaret Sindelar*

PATCHWORK TREE PILLOW

Shown on page 95 *and* 110.
The finished pillow is 15" square.

YOU WILL NEED:

Pattern on page 111

Tracing paper
Assorted white woven-print satin as follows:
½ yard of white woven-print satin
½ yard of white woven-print satin scraps
½ yard of white woven-print satin for piping
White and yellow-gold sewing thread
½ yard of metallic-gold piping and rickrack
¼ yard of off-white woven stripe fabric
18" square of polyester fleece
2 yards of ¼"-diameter cording
Polyester fiberfill
Metallic-silver stem
35 to 40—5mm silver beads
Embroidery needle

INSTRUCTIONS

Note: *Use ½" seam allowances for all stitching, unless otherwise noted.*

Trace the individual patchwork pieces (background pieces 1, 2, 3, and 4 and tree pieces A, B, C, and D) from the pattern onto tracing paper. Add ½" around all of the patchwork pieces for seam allowances. Cut out the pattern pieces.

From the ½ yard of woven-print satin, cut out a 16" square for the pillow back and background pieces 1, 2, 3, and 4. Cut out tree pieces A, B, C, and D from the woven-print satin scraps. Refer to the pillow-assembly

Stitch the pillow front to the back with the right sides facing, leaving an opening for stuffing. Clip the corners, trim the seam allowances, and turn the pillow right side out. Press the pillow, and then stuff firmly with the polyester fiberfill. Hand-sew the pillow opening closed.

Bend the silver-metallic stem into a 1½"-diameter circle, twisting the excess stem around the circle to secure the shape. Hand-sew the circle to the top of the tree. Hand-sew the silver beads to the tree for ornaments.

—Designed by Jim Williams

VINTAGE-LINEN MINI STOCKING

Shown on page 91 *and* below. *The finished stocking is 7¼" tall.*

YOU WILL NEED:

Patterns on page 112

Tracing paper
Scrap of vintage natural linen or cotton fabric
Matching sewing thread
Vintage lace-edged handkerchief
3 vintage ⁷⁄₁₆"-diameter bone buttons
6" length of narrow metallic gold cord
Glue gun and hotmelt adhesive

diagram, *opposite,* to arrange the pieces. Cut the gold piping into one 5½" length and one 9½" length.

With the right sides facing, place and pin the bottom edge of piece A and the top edge of piece B together with the 5½" length of piping between the pieces of fabric. Sew the pieces together. Clip the curve; press.

Pin and stitch the 9½" length of piping to the bottom edge of piece B. With the right sides facing, place and pin the bottom edge of piece B and the top edge of piece C together, with the piping between the pieces of fabric. Sew the pieces together, clip the curve, and press. Referring to the photograph *above,* pin and topstitch a length of rickrack to the tree sections.

Referring to the pillow-assembly diagram and photograph, and with the right sides facing, pin and stitch background pieces 1 and 2 to the pieced tree top. Press the seams open. With the right sides facing, pin and

stitch background pieces 3 and 4 to tree piece D. Press the seams open. With the right sides facing, pin and stitch the two sections together.

From the off-white stripe fabric, cut four 4×16" border strips. With right sides facing, center and pin the strips to the sides of the pieced center, mitering the corners. Stitch the border strips in place, and press.

Pin the pillow front right side up on top of the fleece. With the yellow-gold thread, machine-quilt about ⅜" inside the seam line around all of the background pieces, the four border strips, and piece D.

For the self-covered piping, cut and piece enough 2"-wide bias strips from the piping fabric to cover the cording. Pin and stitch the fabric strip around the cording to complete the piping. With the right sides facing and the raw edges aligned, pin and stitch the piping around the pillow front, rounding the piping at the corners.

PATCHWORK TREE PILLOW PATTERN

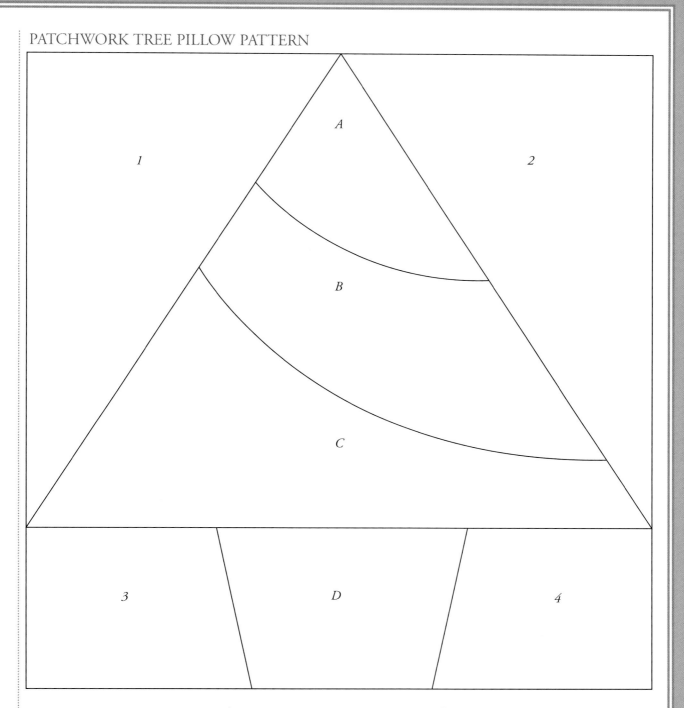

INSTRUCTIONS

Trace the patterns, *page 112,* onto tracing paper. Add a ½" seam allowance around the stocking pattern. Make a mirror image of the cuff pattern, and add a ½" seam allowance to the top and sides. Cut out the pattern pieces.

Cut out a stocking front and back from linen. With right sides together and using a ½" seam allowance, sew around the stocking, leaving the top edge open. Trim the seam allowance, clip the curves, and turn the stocking right side out; press. Topstitch around the stocking. For the cuff, place the tip of the pattern in one decorative corner of the handkerchief. Cut out the cuff front. Repeat for the cuff back. With the right sides facing and using a ½" seam allowance, sew the cuff pieces together along the sides. Trim the seam allowance. Do not turn the cuff right side out. Slip the straight top edge of the cuff inside the stocking for ½". Glue the cuff to the stocking. Fold down the cuff along the dotted line on the pattern piece.

Glue gold cord to the stocking for a hanger; glue buttons down the front.

—*Designed by Jim Williams*

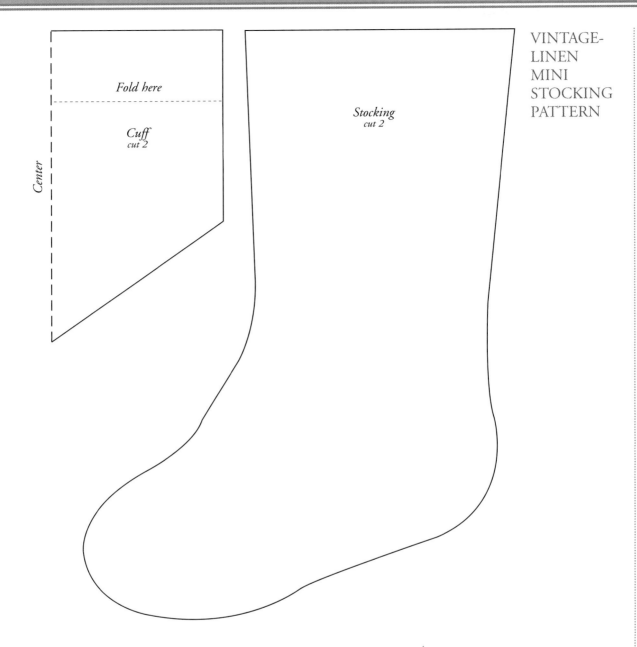

Fold here

Center

Cuff
cut 2

Stocking
cut 2

JINGLE BELL CANDLE SHADE

Shown on page 93 *and* opposite.

YOU WILL NEED:

Scrap of white bias-cut fabric
15 to 18 gold jingle bells
Tube cement
Metal candle shade

INSTRUCTIONS

Note: *Our candle shade is about 4"
tall and 5" in diameter at the base.*

Cut and piece a 1"-wide bias strip
of fabric to measure 18". Fold the
strip in half lengthwise; press. Fold
the long, raw edges to the pressed
fold, and press again to make a ⅜"-
wide strip. Clean-cut one end of the
strip. Glue the end of the bias strip to
the outside of the shade, aligning the
lower edge of the strip with the
bottom edge of the shade. Glue the
end of the strip over the leading edge;
trim excess. Hand-sew bells to strip.

—*Designed by Jim Williams*

PEARS-AND-ROSES WREATH

Shown on page 93 *and* opposite.
The wreath measures 18" in diameter.

YOU WILL NEED:

Louis Nichole's Handy Dandy Decorator™
 Wreath Frame (with corkscrew stems)
Work gloves and pliers
Assorted Christmas greenery
Fresh pears and ivory roses
Several yards of 3"- to 4"-wide gold-edged
 ivory satin ribbon

INSTRUCTIONS

To form the wreath shape, wear work gloves and insert the corkscrew stems onto the wire frame, twisting the stems into the threaded screw holes on the frame. Carefully tighten the stems with pliers.

Twist the pears onto the corkscrew stems around the wire frame. Create a foundation layer of small-leaf greenery by inserting the greenery stems through the frame and around the fresh pears.

Insert fresh roses into the greenery as desired until the arrangement is pleasing to you. If desired, use wooden barbecue skewers to tuck additional pieces of fruit into the areas between the corkscrews.

Wire a ribbon bow and small gold ornaments to the wreath, if desired. When the arrangement is complete, lightly spray-mist it with water to keep the pieces fresh.

MOSAIC BUTTON BALL

Shown on page 90 and below. The finished ornament, without the bow trim, is 3" in diameter.

YOU WILL NEED:

Florist's wire
3"-diameter plastic-foam ball
Scraps of cardboard
White tile adhesive
50 to 60 vintage bone buttons
7" length of narrow metallic-gold cord
1 yard of 1½"-wide gold-edge
  organdy ribbon
Glue gun and hotmelt adhesive
4 small metallic-silver silk leaves
3—½"-diameter metallic-gold Christmas balls
3 silver-painted hemlock pinecones

INSTRUCTIONS

Cut a 7" length of florist's wire for a wire hanger loop. Fold the wire in half, and insert it into the plastic-foam ball. Push the wire through the ball until only about ¼" of the folded end is exposed at the top. (The ends of the wire will stick out through the bottom of the ball.) Twist the exposed ends tightly, and press them into the plastic-foam ball to secure them in place.

Cut the cardboard scraps into 1"-wide strips to use as spreaders for the tile adhesive. Smooth the tile adhesive onto a small portion of the ball, and press the buttons into the adhesive, placing them as close together as possible. Continue in this manner until the entire ball is covered. Set the ball aside to dry, following the tile-adhesive manufacturer's directions.

Slip the metallic-gold cord through the wire hanger loop at the top of the ball. Holding the cut ends of the cord together, tie an overhand knot to form a hanger. Glue the knot to the top of the ornament.

Cut the organdy ribbon into two 18" lengths. Place the ribbon lengths on top of one another. Slip the doubled length of ribbon through the wire hanger loop, and tie it into a bow to cover the knot in the cording hanger. Trim the ends of the ribbon. Secure the bow with glue if necessary.

Glue the metallic-silver leaves, metallic-gold Christmas balls, and silver hemlock pinecones to the front of the bow.

—*Designed by Jim Williams*

TASTES
❧ OF THE SEASON ☙

*A*rrange your holiday

dinner table with hand-painted dinnerware

and ornament favors as well as folded-paper

candleholders and gold-leafed candles.

They'll set the stage for festive holiday desserts.

Our recipes, beginning on page 122, offer

a chocolate raspberry dessert, an eggnog braid, a

cranberry loaf, glacéed pears, and Christmas

cookies for tantalizing treats. (For crafts

instructions, see pages 6–41 and 126–141.)

GLACÉED PEARS

For a quick and delicious dessert, prepare
our mixture of sugar, water, and cream of tartar, and lightly
drizzle it on a pear. Present your creation on top of two stacked
pedestal dishes, garnish it with strawberries, and decorate the
bottom tier with roses for an elegant serving.
Recipe is on page 122.

FESTIVE CRANBERRY LOAF

Cranberry treats are a favorite part of the holiday season.
Make our cranberry loaf part of your holiday tradition—
and pair it with our festive Plaid-Ribbons Dinnerware (see page 29)
for a joyous Christmas celebration. Recipe is on page 125.

CHOCOLATE RASPBERRY DESSERT

An arrangement of ladyfingers wrapped around a chocolate cream filling
and topped with whipped cream and raspberries is an appealing addition to your holiday party
sideboard of dessert selections. Recipe is on page 122.

HOLIDAY EGGNOG BRAID

Form this delicious treat by rolling dough filled with
eggnog, candied fruits, and raisins into three 18"-long ropes and braiding them
together. When the braided loaf has baked, combine powdered sugar and eggnog
to drizzle atop the braid. Recipe is on page 125.

CHRISTMAS COOKIES

HAZELNUT DREAMS COOKIES

Every yummy bite of these Christmas-cookie candy canes is flavorful because our recipe calls for a rich blend of hazelnuts in the cookie dough. Recipe is on page 124.

CHOCOLATE-PEANUT BUTTER PINWHEELS

Roll chocolate and peanut butter cookie dough with semisweet chocolate and chopped peanuts for holiday cookies that are twice the fun and flavor of plain cookies. Recipe is on page 122.

CHRISTMAS STARS

A sprinkling of powdered sugar and a touch of tangy raspberry preserves make these star-shaped cookies a heavenly treat. Recipe is on page 124.

Stack your cookie creations in style on a three-tiered rack, using our hand-painted Plaid-Ribbons Dinnerware for the plates (painting instructions are on page 29).

Make this glacéed pear creation for your holiday dinner table centerpiece.

GLACÉED PEARS

Shown on page 117.
Make this recipe on a nonhumid day when the weather is cold and clear.

YOU WILL NEED:

2 cups sugar
1 cup water
⅛ tsp. cream of tartar
4 to 5 small whole pears

INSTRUCTIONS

Butter a piece of foil and set it aside. Butter the sides of a heavy 2-quart saucepan. Combine sugar, water, and cream of tartar. Cook and stir over medium-high heat to boiling. Clip a candy thermometer to the side of the pan. Cook and stir the mixture over medium-low heat to 310°, hard-crack stage, about 25 to 30 minutes. Remove the mixture from the heat. Quickly drizzle the pears with the syrup using a spoon. Place on the buttered foil to set up.

Note: These do not store well. Serve the same day they are prepared.

CHOCOLATE RASPBERRY DESSERT

Shown on page 118.

YOU WILL NEED:

1 envelope unflavored gelatin
¼ cup cold water
4 oz. semisweet chocolate, chopped
⅓ cup whipping cream
8 to 10 ladyfingers, split in half
1½ cups whipping cream
⅔ cup sifted powdered sugar
1½ tsp. vanilla
Whipped cream
Fresh raspberries or strawberries
Fudge ice-cream topping

INSTRUCTIONS

In a small saucepan combine unflavored gelatin and water; let stand 5 minutes. Cook and stir over low heat until gelatin dissolves. Set mixture aside. In small saucepan melt semisweet chocolate with 3 tablespoons water over low heat. Whisk in ⅓ cup whipping cream until smooth. Stir in gelatin mixture. Remove from heat. Cool to room temperature; stir occasionally.

Meanwhile, line a 1½-quart soufflé dish with plastic wrap. Arrange ladyfinger halves, standing them upright, around the sides of dish; set aside. In a mixing bowl beat 1½ cups whipping cream, powdered sugar, and vanilla until soft peaks form.

Gradually fold the whipping cream mixture into the chocolate mixture. Turn into lined dish; spread the mixture evenly. Cover and chill 4 to 6 hours or until set. To serve, invert the dish and unmold dessert onto a serving platter. Carefully remove the plastic wrap. Garnish dessert with additional whipped cream, fresh raspberries, and fudge ice-cream topping. Makes about 6 to 8 servings.

CHOCOLATE-PEANUT BUTTER PINWHEELS

Shown on pages 120 and 121.

YOU WILL NEED:

1 recipe Chocolate Cookie Dough
1 recipe Peanut Butter Cookie Dough
1 cup semisweet chocolate pieces (optional)
2 tsp. shortening (optional)
1 cup finely chopped peanuts (optional)

Our chocolate raspberry dessert recipe makes about 6 to 8 delicious servings.

Carefully invert one peanut butter rectangle over a chocolate rectangle.

INSTRUCTIONS

Roll each half of Chocolate Cookie Dough between two sheets of waxed paper into a 12×11" rectangle. Repeat with Peanut Butter Cookie Dough.

Place the peanut butter rectangles on baking sheets. Place in the freezer 15 to 20 minutes or until firm. Remove from the freezer. Peel top sheets of waxed paper from all rectangles. Invert one peanut butter rectangle over a chocolate rectangle (see photo *above*).

Remove top sheet of waxed paper. Let stand about 5 minutes or until dough is easy to roll.

Roll up into a spiral, starting from one of the long sides; remove bottom sheet of waxed paper as you roll. Pinch to seal. Cut roll in half crosswise. Wrap each roll in waxed paper or clear plastic wrap. Repeat with remaining chocolate and peanut butter rectangles. Chill about 4 hours or until firm.

Remove one roll from the refrigerator. Unwrap and reshape slightly, if necessary. Cut dough into ¼"-thick slices. Place slices 2" apart on an ungreased cookie sheet.

Bake in a 375° oven 10 to 12 minutes or until edges are firm and bottoms are lightly browned. Cool on cookie sheet 1 minute. Remove to a wire rack; cool completely. Repeat with remaining dough. If desired, melt together chocolate and shortening in a heavy saucepan over low heat. Dip an edge of each cookie into the melted chocolate; sprinkle with nuts. Makes about 90 cookies.

CHOCOLATE COOKIE DOUGH
YOU WILL NEED:

½ cup butter, softened
⅓ cup shortening
1 cup sugar
⅓ cup unsweetened cocoa powder
½ tsp. baking powder
1 egg
2 Tbsp. milk
1 tsp. vanilla
2⅓ cups all-purpose flour

INSTRUCTIONS

In a large mixing bowl, beat butter and shortening with an electric mixer on medium to high speed, for 30 seconds or until softened. Add sugar, cocoa powder, and baking powder; beat until combined. Beat in egg, milk, and vanilla until thoroughly combined. Beat in as much of the flour as you can with the mixer. Stir in any remaining flour with a wooden spoon. Divide dough in half. Cover and chill for about 1 hour or until easy to handle.

PEANUT BUTTER
COOKIE DOUGH
YOU WILL NEED:

½ cup butter, softened
½ cup creamy peanut butter
½ cup granulated sugar
½ cup packed brown sugar
¾ tsp. baking soda
2 eggs
2 Tbsp. milk
1 tsp. vanilla
2½ cups all-purpose flour

INSTRUCTIONS

In a large mixing bowl, beat butter and peanut butter with an electric mixer on medium to high speed for 30 seconds or until softened. Add granulated sugar, brown sugar, and baking soda; beat until combined.

Beat in eggs, milk, and vanilla until thoroughly combined. Beat in flour with the mixer.

Stir in any remaining flour with a wooden spoon.

Divide dough in half. Cover and chill for about 1 hour or until easy to handle.

Tip for Perfect Pinwheels

Chill the top layer of dough in the freezer 15 to 20 minutes or until firm; it will be like stiff cardboard. This will allow you to easily invert the top layer over the bottom layer of dough, lining up the edges.

Let the two layers of dough rest until they are easy to roll, about 5 minutes.

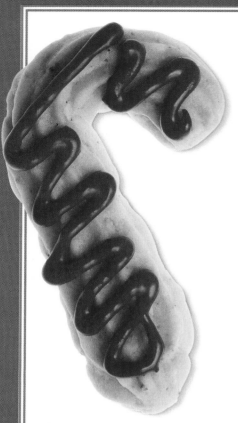

HAZELNUT DREAMS COOKIES

Shown on pages 120 and 121.

YOU WILL NEED:

¾ cup hazelnuts (filberts)
¾ cup butter
½ cup sugar
1 egg
1½ tsp. vanilla
1½ cups all-purpose flour
Candy coating, chopped
Red paste food coloring
Heavy self-sealing plastic bag

INSTRUCTIONS

Spread hazelnuts in a shallow baking pan. Bake in a 325° oven about 15 minutes or until lightly toasted. Cool; rub nuts between hands to remove skins. Place nuts in a food-processor bowl or blender container. Cover and blend or process until finely ground.

In a large mixing bowl with an electric mixer, beat butter on medium to high speed 30 seconds or until softened. Beat in sugar until well combined. Beat in the egg and vanilla. Stir in flour and ground nuts.

Place dough in a pastry bag fitted with a large star tip (about ½" opening). Pipe dough in 2½" lengths onto an ungreased cookie sheet. Bake in a 350° oven about 10 minutes or until edges begin to brown. Cool on wire racks placed over waxed paper.

In a small saucepan over low heat, melt the candy coating. Tint with red paste food coloring. Pour into a heavy self-sealing plastic bag; seal. Cut a small hole in one corner and pipe frosting onto cookies. Let stand until chocolate sets. Makes about 40.

CHRISTMAS STARS

Shown on pages 120, 121, and 125.

YOU WILL NEED:

1½ cups butter, softened
1¾ cups sifted powdered sugar
1 egg
2 cups all-purpose flour
1 cup cornstarch
2 cups walnuts, finely ground
½ cup raspberry preserves (or your favorite)
Powdered sugar

INSTRUCTIONS

In a medium mixing bowl with an electric mixer, beat butter on medium speed 30 seconds. Add 1¾ cups powdered sugar; beat until combined, scraping the bowl. Beat in egg.

In a small bowl, combine flour and cornstarch; add it to the butter mixture. Beat until combined. Stir in finely ground walnuts.

Divide the dough in half. Cover and chill 2 to 3 hours or until firm.

On a lightly floured surface, roll half of the dough at a time to ⅛" thickness. (Keep the remaining dough chilled in the refrigerator until ready to use.)

Cut out cookies with a 3" star-shaped cutter. Cut out a smaller star from the center of half of the cutout star-shaped cookies.

Place cookies on an ungreased cookie sheet. Bake in a 325° oven 12 to 14 minutes or until very lightly browned. Cool on a wire rack.

Carefully spread the solid-star cookies with raspberry preserves. Sift powdered sugar over the star cookies with star cutouts; place them on top of the preserves.

Makes about 30 cookies.

Top our holiday eggnog braid with yummy candied fruits and peels.

HOLIDAY EGGNOG BRAID

Shown on page 119.

YOU WILL NEED:

3 cups all-purpose flour
2 packages active dry yeast
½ tsp. ground nutmeg
1 cup canned or dairy eggnog
¼ cup water
¼ cup butter
¼ cup granulated sugar
1 tsp. salt
1 egg
¾ cup chopped candied fruits and peels
½ cup golden raisins
1 cup sifted powdered sugar
1 to 2 Tbsp. canned or dairy eggnog
Candied fruit (optional)

INSTRUCTIONS

In a large bowl combine 1½ cups flour, yeast, and nutmeg; set aside. In a saucepan, heat and stir the 1 cup eggnog, water, butter, granulated sugar, and salt just until warm (120° to 130°) and the butter almost melts. Add to flour mixture; add egg.

Beat with electric mixer on low to medium speed 30 seconds, scraping bowl. Beat on high 3 minutes.

With wooden spoon, stir in candied fruits and peels, raisins, and as much remaining flour as you can.

Knead in enough remaining flour to make moderately stiff dough that is smooth and elastic (6 to 8 minutes total). Shape into ball. Place in greased bowl; turn once. Cover; let rise in warm place until double (about 1½ hours).

Punch dough down. Turn out onto lightly floured surface. Divide dough into 3 pieces.

Cover; let rest 10 minutes. Roll each piece of dough into an evenly thick 18" rope.

Line up the 3 ropes, 1" apart, on large, greased baking sheet. Starting in middle, loosely braid toward each end. Press ends together to seal; tuck ends under. Cover; let rise until nearly double (about 45 to 60 minutes). Bake in 350° oven 10 minutes. Cover loosely with foil; bake 15 to 20 minutes more, or until bread sounds hollow when lightly tapped. Cool. Combine powdered sugar with eggnog to make drizzling consistency. Drizzle over loaf. Garnish with candied fruit, if desired. Makes 1 loaf.

FESTIVE CRANBERRY LOAF

Shown on page 116.

YOU WILL NEED:

2—3-ounce packages cream cheese, softened
1 egg
2 Tbsp. Cointreau or other orange liqueur or apple juice
1 Tbsp. sugar
2 cups all-purpose flour
1 cup sugar
1½ tsp. baking powder
½ tsp. baking soda
½ tsp. salt
¾ cup apple juice
¼ cup butter, melted
1 beaten egg
1½ cups chopped fresh cranberries
½ cup chopped walnuts

INSTRUCTIONS

Grease and lightly flour a 9×5×3" loaf pan. Set aside.

In a small bowl, beat cream cheese with electric mixer until light and fluffy. Add 1 egg, Cointreau, and 1 tablespoon sugar. Beat until well combined.

In a large bowl, stir together the flour, 1 cup

This loaf has cranberries in every bite.

sugar, baking powder, baking soda, and salt. Stir in apple juice, butter, and beaten egg. Fold in the cranberries and walnuts.

Spoon half of the cranberry batter into the prepared pan. Spoon cream cheese mixture evenly over the batter. Top with the remaining batter.

Bake in a 350° oven 65 to 75 minutes. Cool 15 minutes in the pan on a wire rack.

Remove from pan and cool on rack. When completely cool, wrap tightly in clear plastic wrap.

Store loaf in the refrigerator for up to 1 week, or store in freezer up to 3 months.

Makes one loaf that serves 16.

HOLIDAY
BY CANDLELIGHT

Create a special glow in every corner of the house with hand-decorated candles and candleholders. Our tabletop duo with painted sprigs of holly, *opposite*, sets a festive table top. Also leaf through our pages for cut-paper luminaries, wire-wrapped candleholders, gilded candles, and more. Perfect for gift-giving or for making your own home merry, these are just a few of our brightest ideas.

Instructions begin on page 134.

WIRE-WRAPPED CANDLEHOLDERS

What Christmas crafts decoration could be more simple to make or more stylish to display in so many holiday settings? Start with one or several glass candleholders. Wrap gold crafts wire around the holders. Wrap and twist the wire freely, as shown with our centerpiece, *opposite*, or tightly for a wire motif bow. Whether presented in groupings or individually, these candles will produce a lovely ambiance.

GILDED-PILLAR CANDLES

Add touches of gold leafing to your candles for variety and elegance. Instructions are on page 136.

CHRISTMAS NIGHT LUMINARIES

Transform colored papers into holiday luminaries by folding them into box-shapes, then add mylar "windows" to the sides. Or make unique folded stars for holding small candles. Instructions are on page 134.

HAPPY SNOWMEN CROCK CANDLEHOLDERS

Paint a trio of cheery snowmen motifs on porcelain crocks to hold your favorite candles. Mix and match the designs to make a coordinating set as a gift for your family or friends. Instructions are on page 137.

HOLIDAY STAR AND TREE SCONCES

Cut out these basic wood shapes with a scrollsaw and paint them with acrylics for clever candle sconces. Just trim the wood with wire and secure taper candles. Use them to brightly accent any corner of your home. Instructions are on page 138.

RIBBON-CRAFTS CANDLEHOLDERS

Turn tumblers into fanciful candleholders with varying widths of gold ribbon bands for a dash of decorating whimsy. Instructions are on page 134.

CHRISTMAS-NIGHT LUMINARIES

Shown on page 130.
The Christmas Tree and Star
Candleholders are each 3×3×3½".
The Folded-Star Candleholder
is 6½" in diameter.

YOU WILL NEED:

Patterns opposite *and on* pages 136
and 137

Tracing paper
Scissors
Crafts knife
Heavy red, green, and gold-foil papers
Vellum
Crafts glue
Votive candles

INSTRUCTIONS

Note: *You may choose to use these folded-paper candleholders for decorative purposes only; place lighted candles in glass candleholders.*

Christmas Tree and Star Candleholders

Trace the outline for the box onto tracing paper. Cut out the pattern piece. Trace a tree (or star) on one of the side panels. Use a crafts knife to cut out the design.

Cut the box shape from the heavy red, green, or gold paper. Trace a tree or star on each side panel of the box shape with a pencil. Using the crafts knife, cut out the tree or star shapes. Turn the box shape over and lightly score along the broken lines indicated on the pattern.

Cut four 2¾×3¼" rectangles from the vellum. Apply glue along the outside edges of all vellum rectangles, and adhere them to the wrong sides of the tree and star cutouts.

Fold all the box panels along the scored lines. Apply glue to the side

tab, and press it to the inside of the box. Place glue on the bottom tabs, and glue them to the box bottom. Set a votive candle inside each box.

Folded-Star Candleholder

Trace the outlines of the star patterns onto tracing paper. Cut out the pattern pieces. Cut one large star from heavy red paper and one small star from the heavy gold-foil paper.

Using a crafts knife, lightly score the wrong side of the red star along the broken lines indicated on the pattern. Fold the red star along the scored lines in the sequence indicated by the numbers. Repeat for the gold star.

Place the gold star inside the folded edges of the red star (spot-glue in place, if desired). Set a votive candle on the center of the gold star.

—Designed by Martha Koller Ehrlich

RIBBON-CRAFTS CANDLEHOLDERS

Shown on page 133.

YOU WILL NEED:

Assorted ribbons (in lengths to fit around the outside of the tumblers)
Straight-sided clear glass tumblers
Glue gun and hotmelt adhesive
Votive candles (that fit inside the tumblers)

INSTRUCTIONS

Note: *For the best effect, the tumblers should have straight sides; otherwise the ribbons will not align.*

Select a combination of two, three, or four ribbons to use on each tumbler, and determine their arrangement. Make a straight horizontal cut through one end of the first ribbon; attach the cut edge to the glass with small spots of hot glue.

Wrap the ribbon around the glass to determine the length needed,

allowing ½" for overlap. Cut through the length with a second horizontal cut. Tightly wrap the cut ribbon around the glass; spot-glue in place. Continue adding ribbons, layering some, until the tumbler is covered. Set a votive in the tumbler.

—Designed by Jim Williams

HOLLY HOLIDAY CANDLES

Shown on page 126.

YOU WILL NEED:

Patterns on page 141

DecoArt Americana Acrylic paint: Black Forest Green DA83 (BF), Celery Green DA208 (CG), Glorious Gold DA71 (GG), Light Buttermilk DA164 (LK), White Pearl DA117 (WP), and True Red DA129 (TE)
DecoArt Americana Candle Painting Medium DS39
Palette
Ivory candles: 6"-tall oval and 6"-tall round
Rubbing alcohol
Sponge
Paintbrushes: #4 flat shader and #1 liner
Compressed sponge
Paper towels
Old, scruffy toothbrush
Water container

INSTRUCTIONS

Note: *Mix each acrylic paint with candle-painting medium in a 1:1 ratio. Clean each candle with rubbing alcohol and let dry before applying paint.*

Oval Candle

Sponge GG onto the candle. Lightly sponge WP onto the GG. Use the liner to paint thin GG lines about 1" apart to create bands on the candle. Let dry. Transfer the pattern. Use the flat shader to base-coat the holly leaves CG. Shade BF. Use the liner to outline the leaves BF and paint the

1 square = 1 inch

CHRISTMAS-NIGHT
LUMINARIES PATTERNS

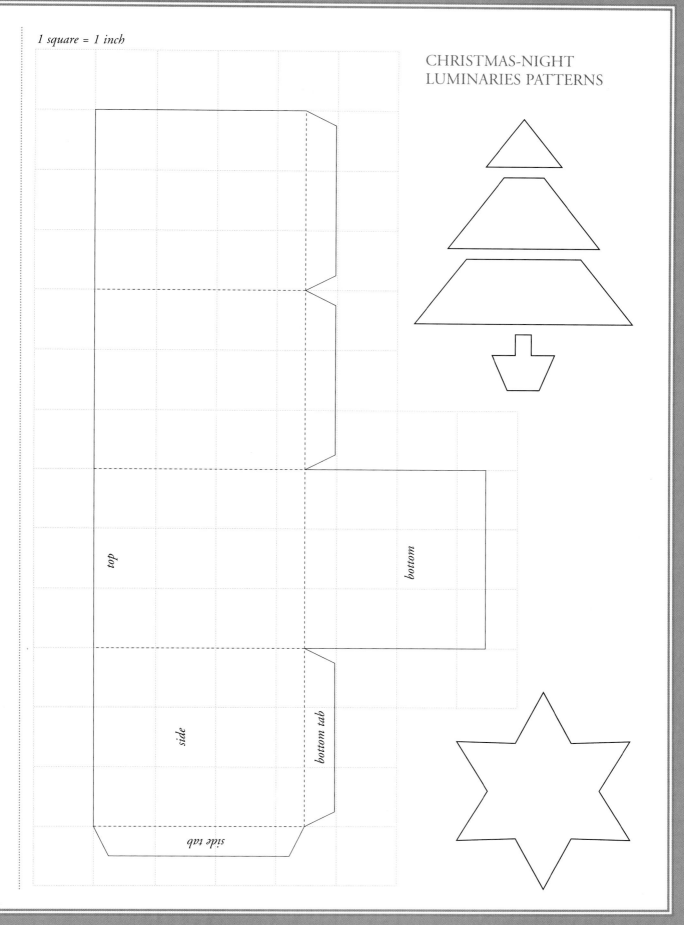

top

bottom

side

bottom tab

side tab

CHRISTMAS-NIGHT LUMINARIES PATTERNS

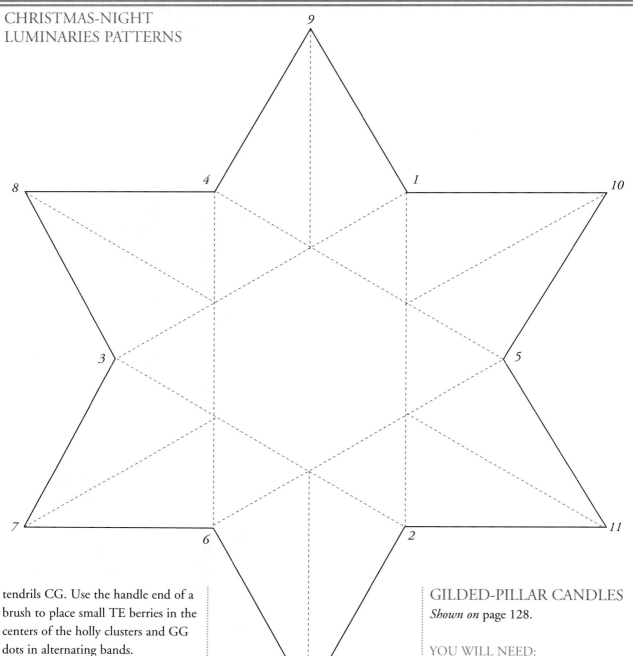

tendrils CG. Use the handle end of a brush to place small TE berries in the centers of the holly clusters and GG dots in alternating bands.

Round Candle
Sponge LK onto the lower half of the candle. Let dry.

Cut the compressed sponge into a holly leaf, and moisten it so it will swell. Place puddles of CG and BF on the palette, press the holly leaf into the paint, and press it on a paper towel to blot out excess paint.

Press the holly-leaf design randomly on the LK areas of the candle,

overlapping some. Use the handle end of a brush to place TE berries among the holly leaves. Let dry. Use the liner to outline and detail the leaves and berries with GG. Dip an old toothbrush into GG thinned with water; spatter the candle with paint.

—*Designed by Teri Stillwaugh*

GILDED-PILLAR CANDLES
Shown on page 128.

YOU WILL NEED:
Masking tape
Pillar candle
½" flat paintbrush
Gold-leaf adhesive
Gold-leaf sheets
Spray matte varnish

INSTRUCTIONS
Firmly press strips of masking tape around the candle horizontally or vertically, as desired. Use the flat brush to apply an even coat of the

CHRISTMAS-NIGHT
LUMINARIES
PATTERNS

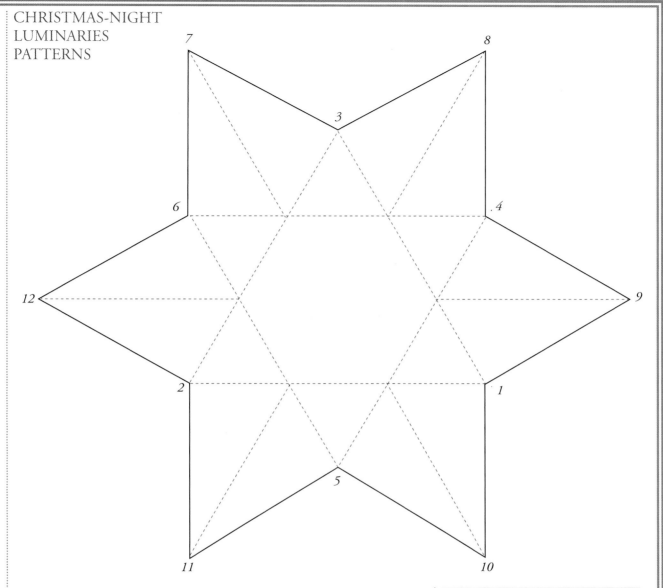

gold-leaf adhesive onto all exposed areas of the candle. Let dry. Apply a second coat of the adhesive. Let dry. Carefully press the gold-leaf sheets onto the exposed areas of the candle, adding additional gold-leaf sheets as necessary. Carefully remove the strips of masking tape. Finish by lightly spraying a coat of varnish on the candle. Let dry.

—*Designed by Ann Blevins*

HAPPY SNOWMEN CROCK CANDLEHOLDERS
Shown on page 131.

YOU WILL NEED:
Patterns on page 139
1—4¾"-diameter natural crock, 5¼" tall (1-quart crock)
2—3¾"-diameter natural crocks, 2" tall (ramekins)
Delta Surface Cleaner and Conditioner
Tracing paper
Transfer paper
Paintbrushes: Flat, round, and liner
Delta PermEnamels paint: Black 2506, Cape Cod 2133 (CC), Chocolate 2021 (DC), Red

Iron Oxide 2020 (RI), and White Retarder (for small crocks only)
Gloss glaze
1—3¾"-diameter candle, 8½" tall
1—2⅞"-diameter candle, 6" tall
1—2¾"-diameter candle, 3" tall

INSTRUCTIONS
Prepare the Crocks
Prepare the crocks with the surface cleaner and conditioner, following the manufacturer's instructions.

Trace the patterns onto tracing paper and transfer them onto the crock using transfer paper. Copy only the outlines of the designs. There's no need to copy details yet—you'd base-coat over them if you did.

Large Snowman Crock

Using the flat brush, base-coat the snowman White, his hat Black, and the hat band and scarf CC.

Scrub the cheeks RI with the round brush. Using the liner, paint the eyes, nose, and mouth Black and the stripes on the scarf White.

Small Crocks

"Welcome Winter" crock: Use the flat brush to paint the snowman White shaded with CC (use the retarder instead of water to thin the CC). Paint the scarf and face as directed above for the snowman on the large crock. With the liner, paint the lettering CC and the twig arms DC with White snow on top.

"Three Little Snowmen" crock: Paint the snowmen as directed above for the *"Welcome Winter"* crock. Add hats as directed above for the large crock.

Finish the Crocks

Use White and the round brush to spatter (flyspeck) snow on all of the crocks. Finish the crocks with two coats of the gloss glaze.

Using the flat brush, paint the sides of the candles CC. Allow the candles to dry. Place the candles in the appropriate crocks.

—*Designed by Pat Olson*

HOLIDAY STAR AND TREE SCONCES

*Shown on page 132 and 133.
The finished star sconce is 7½×10½",
and the tree sconce is 7×11".*

YOU WILL NEED:

Patterns on page 140

For each sconce:
Tracing paper
12" length of 1×8" pine
Scrollsaw, saber saw, or band saw
Drill with ¹³⁄₆₄" and ⅛" bits
100- and 150-grit sandpaper
Disposable sponge paintbrush
Acrylic spray sealer
Wire cutters
Needlenose pliers
2 taper candles (1 old, 1 new)
Wire cutters
For the star sconce:
Gold acrylic paint
Fine-tip black marker
15' length of 16-gauge craft wire
12" length of ½"-diameter wood dowel
For the tree sconce:
Forest green acrylic paint
Copper marker (MinWax detail pen)
18" length of 8-gauge copper wire
14' length of 10-gauge copper wire

INSTRUCTIONS

Note: *Before inserting the candles in the candleholders, be sure the wire holders are positioned so that the candle flame is a safe distance from the wood backing (minimum of 1–1½").*
Enlarge the star and tree patterns onto tracing paper. Cut out the completed pattern pieces.

Draw around the patterns onto the pine. Cut out the shapes with the saw. Drill holes as indicated on the patterns, using the ¹³⁄₆₄" bit for all top (hanger) holes and the candleholder holes on the star. Use the ⅛" bit for the candleholder holes on the tree. Sand all rough edges with 100- and then 150-grit sandpaper.

Paint the star gold and the tree forest green. Let dry, then sand the edges to give the pieces a worn look. Referring to the photograph on *page 133,* use the black marker to outline the edges of the star with wiggly lines

and hash marks. For the tree, draw stars and dots randomly across the surface with the copper marker. Spray both shapes with the acrylic sealer, and allow to dry.

For the star: Fold the 16-gauge wire in half. Secure one end to a doorknob and the other to the length of dowel. Holding the wire taut, rotate the dowel, twisting the doubled length of wire. Twist until you get the desired look, but not to the point when the wire begins to twist back on itself.

Cut an 18" length of the twisted wire for the spiraled V-design at the top of the star. To form a ¾"-diameter spiral at one end of the wire, hold the end tightly with the needlenose pliers and rotate the wire in a circle. As the spiral grows, use your hand to help wind the shape.

Insert the other end through the top hole of the star from the front to the back and form another spiral, this time winding the spiral in the opposite direction. Bend the wire up each side of the star, forming a V-shape. To hang, pound a nail through the back spiral and into the wall.

Insert 1" of the remaining length of twisted wire into the bottom hole. Bend the 1" of wire to meet the back of the star. Wind the wire at the front of the star around an old taper candle until the wire is even with the center hole. Insert the end of the remaining wire through the hole and bend it down to the back of the star. Trim the wire ends, if necessary. Remove the old candle and insert a new one.

For the tree: Insert the end of the 8-gauge wire into the bottom hole. Bend about 2" of wire up on the back side. On the front, wrap the wire around an old taper candle twice, then insert the wire end into the center hole. Bend about 1" of wire

HAPPY SNOWMEN
CROCK CANDLEHOLDERS
PATTERNS

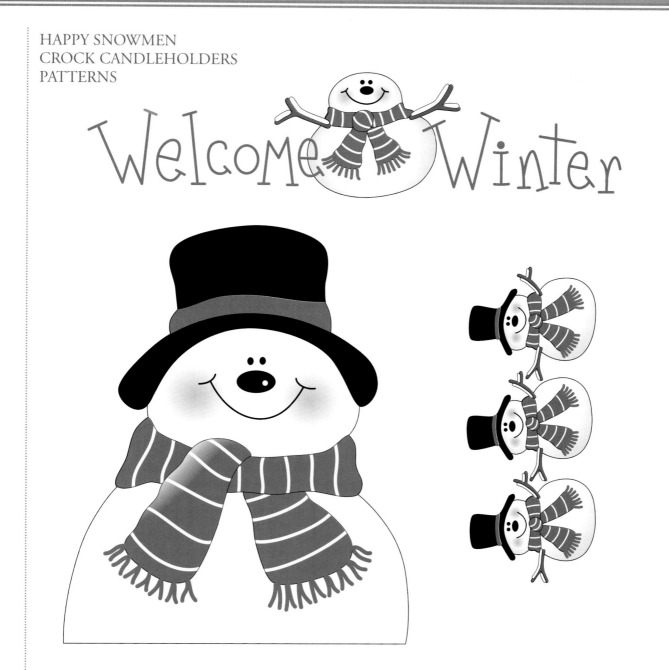

Welcome Winter

down on the back of the tree, and then remove the candle.

Twist one end of the 10-gauge wire around the 8-gauge wire on the back of the tree. Bring the wire to the front of the tree around the bottom, and then begin wrapping it diagonally around the branches up to the top of the tree. Wrap the wire in the same manner back down the tree, creating a crisscross design on the front. Twist the end of the wire to

the 8-gauge wire on the back side of the tree, and cut away any remaining length of the 10-gauge wire.

Cut four 8" lengths of the 10-gauge wire. Make a spiral at each end of the wire as directed for the star, turning the second spiral in the opposite direction to form an S shape.

Cut two 6" lengths of the 10-gauge wire. Form a spiral at one end and a loop at the opposite end of each piece. Hang the S shapes and the

single spirals on the crossed wires.

Cut a 12" length of the 10-gauge wire. Form a ¾"-diameter spiral at one end of the wire. Insert the other end through the top hole of the tree from the front to the back and form another spiral, winding it in the opposite direction. Bend the wire on each side of the tree to form a V-shape. Insert a new taper.

—Designed by Barbara Matthiessen

HOLIDAY TREE AND STAR
SCONCE PATTERNS

1 square = 1 inch

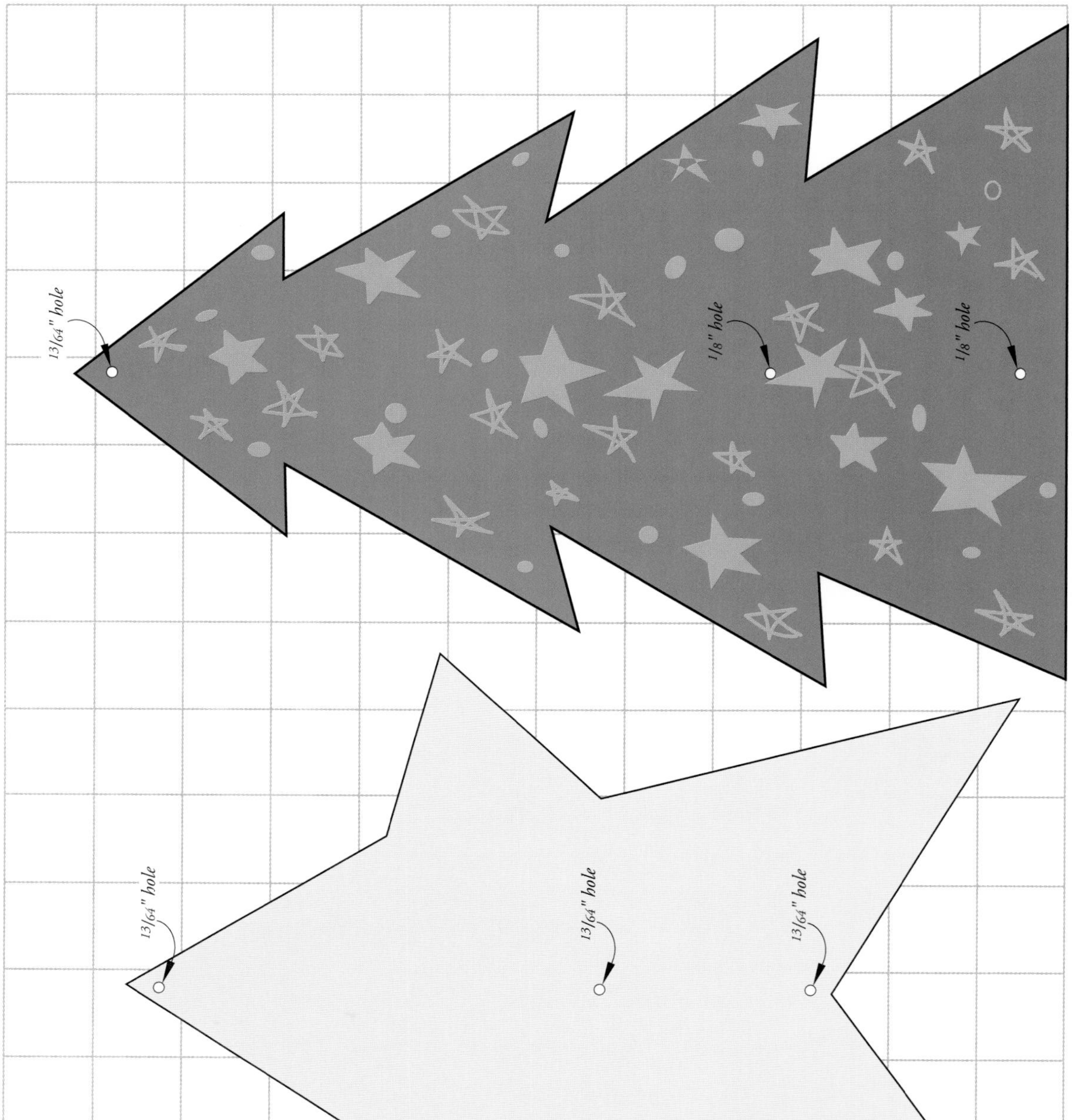

13/64" hole

1/8" hole

1/8" hole

13/64" hole

13/64" hole

13/64" hole

HOLLY HOLIDAY
CANDLES PATTERNS

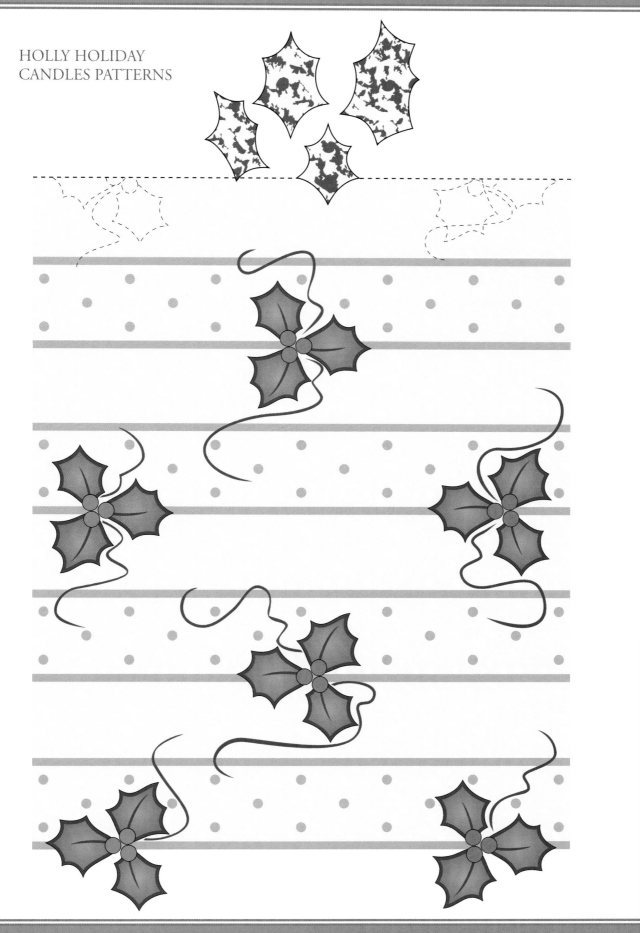

FUN FOR THE FAMILY

We include projects in this section that are perfect for family get-togethers. Use star stickers—like the ones your kids receive on their best schoolwork—to decorate cards. Include your kids in projects to stamp snowman designs onto gift wrappings, and craft an easy folded-paper garland. And your kids will love signing their names for a message to Santa on a painted cookie plate. Instructions begin on page 148.

HOLIDAY STAR CARDS

Kids will love to apply metallic star stickers onto
folded index cards to make these festive Christmas cards.
Simply trace holiday cookie cutter shapes on the cards
for the templates, then fill in the designs with
creative sticker arranging. Instructions are on page 149.

SANTA'S COOKIE PLATE

One popular Christmas tradition involves leaving cookies and
milk for Santa and carrots for his reindeer. Begin your own tradition
by painting this charming plate with a "Dear Santa" message, and
then enjoy displaying the plate for many Christmases to come.
Instructions are on page 148.

EASY FOLDED-PAPER GARLAND

Your kids can help you collect lots of colored and patterned papers to make a folded-paper garland for a table top tree. Once you've learned the steps, show your kids how to create sections of the garland, and they'll eagerly add more chains. Instructions are on page 148.

STAMPED GOODIES BAG AND WRAP

Stamp this cheery snowman on gift wrap and boxes to brighten holiday spirits. Remember to add dots of falling snow to complete the winter scene. Instructions are on page 149.

SANTA'S COOKIE PLATE

Shown on page 145.

YOU WILL NEED:

Patterns at right *and* opposite

Disposable sponge brush

Oak color wood stain

Walnut Hollow Wooden Plate 3526

Stencil acetate

X-ACTO knife or crafts knife

Plaid FolkArt Acrylic paint: Licorice 938 (LI),
  Napthol Crimson 435 (NC), Nutmeg 944
  (NU), Teddy Bear Brown 417 (TD), and
  Wicker White 901 (WW)

Spray stencil adhesive

Paintbrushes: Stencil, #1 liner, and sponge

Tracing paper and transfer paper

Medium-point black permanent marker

Satin finish varnish

INSTRUCTIONS

Note: *This painted wood surface is for decorative purposes only. Serve food on a glass plate placed on the painted piece.*

Use a sponge brush to apply a coat of wood stain to the plate. Let dry.

Trace and transfer the patterns onto the stencil acetate and cut them out with the X-ACTO knife. Spray stencil adhesive to the back of the stencils, and position them on the plate rim. Stencil the gingerbread people TD and the hearts NC. Let dry.

Trace and transfer the patterns for the lettering to the center of the plate and the faces onto the gingerbread people. Thin WW with water to ink consistency, and use the liner to paint the letters and the arms and legs frosting trim on the gingerbread people. Thin LI with water to ink consistency, and use the liner to paint the mouths and eyes. Paint the bows NC. Using the handle end of the brush, dot each letter with WW and the eyes with LI. Let dry. Sign the plate with the marker. Let dry. Apply satin-finish varnish. Let dry.

—Designed by Ann Blevins

SANTA'S COOKIE PLATE PATTERNS

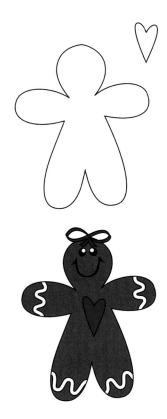

EASY FOLDED-PAPER GARLAND FOLDING DIAGRAMS

Note: *Fold the paper as indicated by the direction of the arrows.*

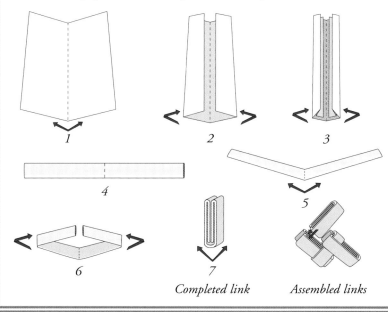

1

2

3

4

5

6

7

Completed link   *Assembled links*

EASY FOLDED-PAPER GARLAND

Shown on page 146.

YOU WILL NEED:

54 to 60—2×3" color images cut
 from magazines

Straightedge

X-ACTO knife or crafts knife

Cutting mat

INSTRUCTIONS

Note: *Adults should cut out the magazine pieces; kids love folding the pieces to make the garland.*

Select brightly colored magazine photos from articles and advertisements. Look for a series of related colors that have little or no writing on them. With a straightedge and an X-ACTO knife, cut the

SANTA'S COOKIE
PLATE PATTERNS

Dear Santa. Here's some cookies just for you. And a carrot for Rudolph too.

photos into 2×3" pieces.

Note: *Always fold the rectangles of paper lengthwise and make the folds crisp so your garland will be successful.*

Refer to the folding diagrams, *opposite,* to make a link of the chain. Repeat the folding process with a second piece of paper to create the second link of the chain.

To assemble the pieces, slip the two folded edges of the first link between the two folded edges of the second link to make a V shape (see the bottom right diagram, *opposite*).

Fold a third piece of paper as described above, and insert it into the second link of the chain.

Continue folding and inserting links in this manner until you are satisfied with the length of your garland.

—*Designed by Jim Williams*

STAMPED GOODIES BAG AND WRAP

Shown on page 147.

YOU WILL NEED:

Posh Impressions Stamps: "Snappy
  Snowman" Z433 and "Let It Snow" Z505
Felt-tip markers and white paper
Color Box ink pads in desired colors
Gift bag or box
Posh Impressions Foam Dots (for 3D mounts)

INSTRUCTIONS

Referring to the photograph on *page 147,* color in the snowman stamp image with markers. Press the stamp on the paper and cut it out.

Randomly stamp the snowflakes image onto a bag or box. Adhere the snowman onto the bag or box with the foam dots for 3D mounting.

—*Designed by Ann Blevins*

HOLIDAY STAR CARDS

Shown on pages 142 *and* 144.

YOU WILL NEED:

1 package of 4×6" blank index cards
Christmas cookie cutters for stencil templates
Pencil
1 package of multi-color foil stars (gummed or
  self-adhesive)

INSTRUCTIONS

Note: *Young children (up to 5 or 6 years old) may need assistance tracing around the cookie cutters.*

Fold the index cards in half. Using the cookie cutters, outline the shapes with a pencil on the front of the cards. (Use a square shape for the gift box design.) Fill in the shapes with different-colored star stickers. Erase any pencil outlines as necessary.

—*Designed by Helena Owens*

LAST-MINUTE GIFTS

*L*ooking for a quick gift to give?
Sometimes a package can be a treat in itself.
Make our quick and easy gift boxes in four styles,
and fill them with goodies. Paint a papier-mâché
box to display a Merry Christmas wish, *opposite*.
Wrap ribbons around a music box to make a
package in tune with your creativity. Punch a
holiday message on a tin-topped box. Paint a
cheery snowman on a country bucket.
Instructions begin on page 154.

MERRY MELODIES MUSIC BOX

Wrap sheer green and red ribbons in a plaid pattern to turn a wooden music box into a beautiful gift. Gathered ribbon flowers clustered on the lid and pretty ribbon bows add an elegant finishing touch. Instructions are on page 155.

SNOWMAN GIFT BUCKET

Present this hand-painted tote loaded with goodies to the host at your next holiday party. Once the treats are gone, the cheery snowman-motif bucket makes a great display piece throughout the season. Instructions are on page 157.

TRIM-THE-TREE BOX

Try an easy tin-punch project. Use a hammer and an awl to tap the phrase "Trim the Tree" into a piece of lightweight tin. Mount the work onto a hand-painted papier-mâché box adorned with a homespun fabric bow. Instructions are on page 157.

COUNTRY CABIN BOX PATTERN

COUNTRY CABIN BOX
Shown on page 150 *and below.*
The box with the lid measures 5×7".

YOU WILL NEED:
Pattern opposite

Paintbrushes: Loew-Cornell 1" flat; #12 flat, #1 round, liner, and spatter or old toothbrush

5×7" lidded papier-mâché box

Delta Ceramcoat Acrylic paint: Antique Gold 2002 (AN), Autumn Brown 2055 (AB), Black 2506, Cinnamon 2495 (CM), Light Ivory 2401 (LI), Pine Green 2526 (PN), Red Iron Oxide 2020 (RI), and Trail Tan 2435 (TR)

Tracing paper

Antiquing medium

Matte spray finish

Spray or brush-on varnish

INSTRUCTIONS
Using the 1" flat brush, base-coat the base of the box and the lid TR.

Trace the pattern onto tracing paper, and transfer it to the top of the lid. Copy only the basic outlines of the pattern to the lid. There's no need to copy the details yet—you'll base-coat over them.

To paint the design, base-coat areas of color with the flat paintbrushes, using the size that best fits the area. Apply details with the liner brush. Base-coat the snow LI, the house and chimneys RI, the roof Black, the tree trunks and branches AB, the needles PN, and the stars AN. Float-shade the house CM and the stars RI.

Paint the lettering and the wreath PN. Add dots and a bow to the wreath with AN. Add RI dots to the ends of the tree branches. Paint the door and windows Black.

Using the #12 flat brush, paint the blocks around the lip of the lid Black.

Using the spatter or old toothbrush, lightly spatter the lid and the base of the box Black. Let the box dry. Brush on antiquing medium; let dry.

Spray the finished piece with the matte finish; cover with one or two coats of varnish.

—Designed by Pat Olson

MERRY MELODIES MUSIC BOX
Shown on page 152 *and above.*

YOU WILL NEED:
4½×3×2½" Walnut Hollow wooden box and music works

Spray acrylic sealer

Bucilla organza ribbons: 2.7mm Mauve 0519, Pink 0507, Tan 0521, and Ivory 0514; 2.3mm Hunter Green 9011; and 1.4mm Red 1504

Plaid Gloss Lustre Mod Podge

Disposable foam brush

Crafts glue; glue gun and hotmelt adhesive

Moire taffeta lining fabric (optional)

½ yard of Bucilla variegated ribbon: 1.4mm Christmas Red 135

Red sewing thread and sewing needle

3 artificial silver flower stamens

INSTRUCTIONS
Spray the box inside and out with the acrylic sealer. Set the box aside.

Plan the arrangement of organza ribbons for the plaid design with the bottom layer consisting of horizontal

SNOWMAN GIFT BUCKET PATTERN

Snowman's left arm

Snowman's right arm

ribbons and the top layer vertical ribbons. Brush Mod Podge on the lid, and when the medium begins to get tacky, apply the layer of horizontal ribbons over the lid, smoothing them from side to side. Let dry. Apply Mod Podge over the lid again, and in the same manner apply the remaining ribbons from front to back. Also add a length of ribbon around all four sides of the lid. Let dry.

Apply two more coats of the Mod Podge to the lid, letting the medium dry between coats. **Note:** *Prop the lid open with foil to avoid sealing it closed while applying Mod Podge.*

Glue a band of ribbon around the feet of the box. Apply Mod Podge to the box sides and bottom. Line the box with the taffeta fabric, if desired.

Install the music works, following the manufacturer's instructions.

For each flower, cut a 5½"-long piece of the variegated ribbon. Work gathering stitches around three sides of the ribbon, leaving one long edge ungathered. Pull the thread tightly to gather the stitches, coiling the ribbon around itself as you gather; secure with backstitches. Make three flowers. Glue stamens to the center of each flower. Tie two or three bows from the desired organza ribbons. Adhere the bows and flowers to the lid.

—Designed by Margaret Sindelar

SNOWMAN GIFT BUCKET
Shown on page 153 *and* left.

YOU WILL NEED:
Pattern opposite
8½×12×9" wooden bucket
Tracing paper and medium-grit sandpaper
White transfer paper
Delta Ceramcoat Acrylic paint: Bittersweet 2041 (BT), Black 2506, Cloudberry 2112 (CD), Magnolia White 2487 (MW), Nightfall 2131 (NF), Palomino 2108 (PA), Red Iron Oxide 2020 (RI), and Straw 2078 (SW)
Paintbrushes: Loew Cornell 1"-wide flat, #10 or #12 flat, #3 round, liner, old toothbrush
Spray acrylic paint and spray varnish

INSTRUCTIONS
Trace the pattern onto tracing paper. Sand the bucket smooth, then use the widest flat brush to base-coat the bucket NF. Allow to dry. Paint the wood handle PA.

Center and transfer the basic outlines of the design to the bucket. Don't copy the details yet—you'll base-coat over them. Base-coat areas of color with the flat paintbrushes, using the size that best fits the area. Apply details with the liner brush. Base-coat the snowman MW, the hat and twig arms Black, the scarf CD, and the nose BT. Base-coat the star MW, then base-coat it SW. Paint the scarf stripes and float-shade the star RI. Paint the snow on the twig arms and the star hanging loop MW. Paint the eyes and mouth Black. Spatter snow over the snowman using the spatter or old toothbrush and MW. Allow to dry; varnish.

—Designed by Pat Olson

TRIM-THE-TREE BOX
Shown on page 152 *and* below.

YOU WILL NEED:
Pattern on page 158
Apple-cider vinegar
Metal jelly roll pan
1 sheet of Quick-Rust™ Steel
7½×5" papier-mâché box
Sponge brush and ¾" stencil brush
Green, cream, dusty-blue, and white acrylic paint
Straight scissors
Pinking shears
Tracing paper and tape
Scrap of soft pine
Hammer and awl or ⅟₃₂" nail set
Permanent black marking pen
Graphite paper and stylus
28-gauge wire
Polyester fiberfill
Disappearing-ink pen
Glue gun and hotmelt adhesive
36×½" strip of checked fabric
2—2-hole red buttons (½" and ¾" in diameter)

INSTRUCTIONS
Pour apple-cider vinegar into the jelly roll pan. **Note:** *Don't use an enamelware or glass, plastic, or Teflon-coated pan.* Immerse a sheet of Quick-Rust Steel in the vinegar and soak for 20 to 30 minutes. Stand the steel on edge to dry.

The steel rusts as it air-dries, which can take 1 to 3 hours, depending on the humidity. When the steel is dry, it is a copper color with uneven streaks and swirls. For heavier rust, spray both sides of the steel with water, and let it dry again.

Use a sponge brush to paint the outside of the box bottom green and the outside of the lid cream.

Cut a 4½×6½" piece of the rusted steel with the pinking shears. Copy the pattern onto tracing paper, and tape it to the steel.

Lay the steel on a scrap of pine, and use a hammer and an awl or nail set to pierce each dot of the lettering only. If the steel curls, turn it over and lightly hammer over the punched holes to flatten it.

Remove the pattern, and cut out the tree and ornament shapes with straight scissors. Trace the tree and

ornament onto another piece of rusted steel and cut them out.

Dip the stencil brush into green paint, wipe off most of the paint on a paper towel, and dab color on the tree. Apply the paint lightly so the rust still shows through in some places. Paint the bottom of the ornament white and the top dusty-blue. Let the paint dry.

To attach the ornament to the rusted-steel rectangle, position the shape on the steel, then lay the pieces on the pine scrap; punch two holes in the center with the hammer and awl. Center the small button on the ornament. "Sew" the button to the rectangle through all of the layers using the 28-gauge wire; twist the wire on the back to secure in place.

Position the tree on the steel rectangle, then lay the pieces on the pine scrap. Punch holes around the

perimeter of the tree through both layers of steel as described for the lettering. Sew the two pieces of steel together with the wire, stuffing the tree with fiberfill before sewing completely around the shape. Use a dull knife to maneuver the fiberfill.

Center the steel on the box lid, and trace around it with the disappearing-ink pen. Remove the steel and, working quickly, apply hotmelt adhesive just inside the traced line. Reposition the steel on the lid, and hold it firmly on all sides until the glue dries.

Wrap a 20"-long piece of checked fabric around the box bottom, and secure it with hotmelt adhesive. Make a bow with the rest of the fabric, and attach it to the front of the box with the adhesive. Add the remaining button to the middle of the bow.

—*Designed by Nancy Hughes*

TRIM-THE-TREE BOX PATTERN

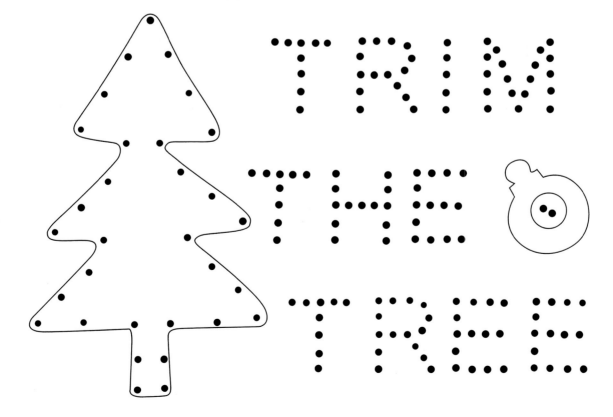

STITCHING BASICS

SINGLE CROCHET

Illustration A: At the beginning of a row, insert your crochet hook into the second chain from the hook.

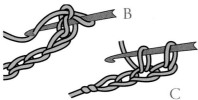

Illustrations B and C: Slip the hook under the yarn, and then use the hook to pull it through the chain. This is called yarn over (or yarn over hook) and is abbreviated as "yo". There are two loops on the hook.

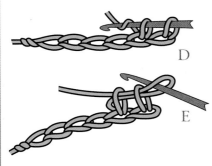

Illustrations D and E: Yarn over again, then pull the loop completely through the two loops on the hook. You have just completed a single crochet. To work the next single crochet, insert your hook into the next chain, and repeat steps B-E.

DOUBLE CROCHET

Illustration A: At the beginning of a row, slip the hook under the yarn (yarn over), and insert the hook into the fourth chain from the hook.

Illustration B: Yarn over again, and pull the loop through the stitch. Notice that there are three loops on the hook.

Illustration C: Yarn over, and pull the loop completely through the first two loops on the hook. Notice that two loops remain on the hook.

Illustrations D and E: Yarn over once more, and pull the loop through the remaining two loops on the hook. One loop remains on the hook. You have just completed a double crochet. To work the next double crochet, yarn over and insert your hook into the next chain; repeat steps B-E.

CROSS-STITCH

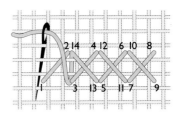

Make one cross-stitch for each symbol on the chart. On most linen and evenweave fabrics, work your stitches over two threads as shown *above*. For Aida cloth, each stitch should fill one square.

BACKSTITCH

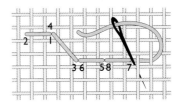

Most cross-stitch projects require only one ply of floss for backstitches. On the color key, (2X) indicates that you should use two plies of floss, (3X) indicates three plies, and so forth.

FRENCH KNOT

Bring the threaded needle through the fabric, and wrap the floss around the needle as shown in the diagram *above*. Tighten the wraps, and return the needle through the fabric in the same place. The floss will slide through the wrapped thread to make the knot.

SOURCES

Look for supplies to make our projects at arts, crafts, fabric, and needlecrafts stores, or contact these companies for more information.

CRAFTS

Cabin Craft Southwest (MUD antiquing medium),
P.O. Box 876, Bedford, TX 76095, orders only: 800/877-1515.

Cabin Crafters (wood cutouts),
1225 W. First St., Nevada, IA 50201, 800/669-3920.

C. M. Offray (ribbons),
Rte. 24, Box 601, Chester NJ 07930, 908/879-4700.

The Caron Collection (floss),
55 Old South Ave., Stratford, CT 06615, 203/381-9999.

Coffee Break Designs (snaps),
P.O. Box 34281, Indianapolis, IN 46234, 317/290-1542.

Down Memory Lane (7½×5" papier-mâché box and Quick Rust™ Steel),
715 Carroll St., Boone, IA 50036, 515/432-3222.

Homespun Touch (crocks, wooden bucket, and 5×7" papier-mâché box),
231 N. 7th Ave., Sturgeon Bay, WI 54235, 800/445-5753.

Louis Nicole (wreath form),
105 E. 29th St., New York, NY 10016, 212/685-0395.

Posh Impressions (rubber stamps),
4708 Barranca Pkwy., Irvine, CA 92604, 800/421-7674.

Rubber Stampede (rubber stamps),
967 Stanford Ave., Oakland, CA 94608, 800/632-8386.

Sakura of America (Pigma pens),
30780 San Clemente St., Hayward, CA 94544, 800/776-6257.

Silkpaint Corporation (Fiber-Etch fabric remover),
P.O. Box 18, Waldron, MO 64092, 816/891-7774.

Walnut Hollow (wood products),
1409 State Rd. 23, Dodgeville, WI 53533, 608/935-2341.

NEEDLEWORK

Anchor (embroidery floss),
Consumer Services Dept., P.O. Box 27067, Greenville, SC 29616.

Bucilla (silk ribbon),
1 Oak Ridge Rd., Hazelton, PA 18201, 717/384-2525.

DMC (embroidery floss),
10 Port Kearny, S. Kearny, NJ 07032, 973/589-0606.

Gay Bowles Sales/Mill Hill (beads)
P.O. Box 1060, Janesville, WI 53547, 608/754-9466.

JHB International (buttons),
1955 S. Quince St., Denver, CO, 80231, 303/751-8100.

Needleworker's Delight (embroidery fabrics)
800/931-4545.

Wichelt Imports (embroidery fabrics),
Embroidery Services Department, P.O. Box 139, Stoddard, WI 54658.

PAINTING

Binney and Smith (Liquitex paint),
1100 Church Ln., Easton, PA 18042, 610/253-6271.

DecoArt (paint),
P.O. Box 386, Stanford, KY 40484, 800/367-3047.

Delta Technical Coatings (paint),
2550 Pellissier Place, Whittier, CA 90601-1505, 800/423-4135.

Duncan Enterprises (paint),
5673 E. Shields Ave., Fresno, CA 93727, 559/291-4444.

Jo Sonja/Chroma (paint),
205 Bucky Dr., Lititz, PA 17543, 800/257-8278.

Loew-Cornell (paintbrushes),
563 Chestnut Ave., Teaneck, NJ 07666-2490, 201/836-7070.

Plaid Enterprises (paint),
P.O. Box 2835, Norcross, GA 30091, 800/842-4197.

CONTRIBUTING PHOTOGRAPHERS

Craig Anderson: Pages 47–48, 129, and 145.

Marcia Cameron: Pages 7, 9–10, 19, 53, and 152.

Hopkins Associates: Pages 88, 90–93, 96–97, and 130.

Scott Little: Pages 13, 20–21, 42, 45, 51–52, 74, 77, 80, 95, 98–99, 131, 146, and 150.

Perry Struse: Pages 11–12, 15–16, 46, 49–50, 94, 114, 116–119, 121, 132, and 153.

Steve Struse: Pages 82–83, 126, and 142.

CONTRIBUTING FOOD STYLIST

Jill Mead: Pages 114, 116–117, 118–119, and 121.